A HANDBOOK FOR CHURCHWARDENS AND PAROCHIAL CHURCH COUNCILLORS

Other Mowbray Parish Handbooks

Handbook for Council and Committee Members
Gordon W. Kuhrt
Handbook of Parish Finance, *3rd edition*
Phyllis Carter and Michael Perry
Handbook of Parish Preaching
Gordon W. Ireson
Handbook of Parish Worship, *new edition*
Michael Perry and Chris Newlands
Handbook of Parish Youth Work
Clive Andrews
Handbook of Pastoral Work
Michael Hocking
Handbook of Sick Visiting
Norman Autton

In preparation

An ABC for the PCC, *3rd edition*
John Pitchford
Adult Way to Faith: a practical handbook with resources to photocopy
Peter Ball
Handbook of Fundraising
Martin Field and Gill Moody
Yours, Lord: a Handbook of Christian Stewardship
Michael Wright

A HANDBOOK FOR

CHURCHWARDENS AND PAROCHIAL CHURCH COUNCILLORS

by

KENNETH M. MACMORRAN

Q.C., M.A., LL.B.

Formerly Chancellor of the Dioceses of
Chichester, Lincoln, Ely, St Albans, Newcastle and Guildford

E. GARTH MOORE

M.A., D.C.L.

Formerly of Gray's Inn, Barrister-at-Law
Chancellor of the Dioceses of Durham, Southwark and Gloucester
Clerk in Holy Orders
Fellow of Corpus Christi College, Cambridge

and

TIMOTHY J. BRIDEN

M.A., I.L.B.

Of the Inner Temple
Barrister-at-Law

MOWBRAY

Mowbray
A Cassell imprint
Villiers House, 41/47 Strand, London WC2N 5JE, England

First published in November 1921
New edition, 1957
New edition, 1966
New edition, 1971
Thirty-seventh impression, revised, 1973
Thirty eighth impression 1975
New edition, 1977
New edition, 1978
New edition, 1980
Reprinted with amendments, 1982
Reprinted, with further amendments, 1983
Forty-fourth impression, 1985
New edition, 1986
New edition, 1989
Reprinted 1990, 1991, 1992, 1993, 1994

ISBN 0-264-67289-5

Typeset by Fakenham Photosetting Limited
and printed and bound in Great Britain by
Biddles Limited, Guildford and King's Lynn

Contents

Introduction

For most church people in England, the parish is the unit which most closely affects them, and in 1921 its government was drastically revised by the passing in that year of the Parochial Church Councils (Powers) Measure. Chancellor Macmorran was quick to realise the need created by that Measure for a simple guide for those concerned with its implementation, namely, churchwardens and parochial church councillors (and he might equally have included incumbents and assistant curates). So he wrote the first edition of this book. How right was his perception of the need is evidenced by the number of further editions and impressions which have ensued. Ever since that first edition there has been a steady increase in the importance of the parochial church council as an element in the government of the Church of England. At the same time, the body of legislation imposing responsibilities upon the council has grown to substantial proportions. Further expansion of the text has now been made necessary by the implementation of the Patronage (Benefices) Measure 1986, parts of which are printed in Chapter 6. It is hoped that the current edition, like its predecessors, will provide assistance to those whose task is to understand and apply that part of ecclesiastical law which touches on parish affairs.

E. Garth Moore
Timothy Briden

December 1988

1

The Constitution of the Church

(1) The Province—(2) The Diocese—(3) The Archdeaconry—(4) The Rural Deanery—(5) Synodical Government: (a) Historical Background; (b) The General Synod; (c) Diocesan Synods; (d) Deanery Synods.

(1) THE PROVINCE

The Province of Canterbury, consisting of thirty[1], and the Province of York, consisting of fourteen, dioceses, together constitute the Church of England as far as this country is concerned. With the other Churches in communion with the See of Canterbury and the overseas provinces this work is not concerned. Each of the Provinces of Canterbury and York is under the direction of an archbishop, and both the archbishops preside over dioceses as well as exercising their archi-episcopal authority in their respective provinces.

An archbishop is president of his convocation and he issues his mandate for the assembly of that body on receipt of a writ from the Crown. During a vacancy in the see of a

[1] The thirtieth being the new diocese of Europe, incorporated into England (for ecclesiastical purposes) in 1980. For obvious reasons, its constitution cannot wholly accord with that of the other dioceses, and this book omits further reference to it. Sodor and Man and that part of the diocese of Winchester which comprises the Channel Islands also provide special cases with which this book does not deal.

diocese within the province he provides for the ecclesiastical administration of that diocese in his capacity of 'guardian of the spiritualities'[1] for the whole province. He normally nominates a suffragan or assistant bishop for the purpose. It is his duty to consecrate new bishops, including suffragan bishops, although his participation in the consecration is not necessary to its validity. A bishop holding office within the province swears an oath of canonical obedience to the archbishop.

The Archbishops of Canterbury and York have the special styles respectively of Primate of All England and Metropolitan, and Primate of England and Metropolitan. Both of them are always members of the House of Lords.

(2) THE DIOCESE

The diocese is a defined territory presided over by a bishop, who has an exclusive jurisdiction within it. In some statutes and in the Prayer Book, the bishop is spoken of as the 'ordinary', i.e. as having ordinary jurisdiction in ecclesiastical matters within his diocese. This denotes as resident in the diocesan an original as distinct from a delegated jurisdiction.

The principle which underlies the whole system of the spiritual government of the Church is that of vesting the government of each diocese in the bishop of that diocese. This dominant idea is to be seen in actual working every day. Thus no bishop may presume to exercise any episcopal function in the diocese of another without the consent of the diocesan, and he may be inhibited from so doing.

[1] A vacant arch-see is administered by the dean and the chapter. In the case of several of the more ancient dioceses, when there is a vacancy in the see, it is customary for the archbishop to delegate the guardianship to the dean and chapter of the cathedral church of the diocese. The Dean and Chapter of Durham claim to be the guardians of spiritualities of that diocese during a vacancy. The claim is not admitted by the Archbishop, but in fact it is the Dean and Chapter who act.

Again, the diocesan bishop institutes an incumbent to his cure, and that incumbent has no rights in his parish until the institution has taken place. Nor has an assistant curate any rights in his office until he has been licensed by the bishop. Nor can a layman take upon himself the office of reader without the bishop's permission.

At the same time, the Anglican episcopate is a constitutional episcopate and not an absolutely monarchical one. In this respect the bishop is bound in several ways. He is the centre and head of his diocese, and the unity of the Church requires that this should be so. But at his consecration he takes an oath of obedience to the archbishop, and he is bound to govern his diocese in accordance with the law of the Church.

It is, perhaps, hardly necessary to add that in ruling his diocese, a bishop must conform to the secular law so far as it is applicable. His duties are regulated in innumerable matters by common law and statute, and so far as these are of intimate concern to the laity, mention is made of them in their appropriate context in the chapters which follow.

In addition to the two archbishops, the Bishops of London, Durham and Winchester, together with twenty-one other diocesan bishops according to seniority of appointment as diocesans, have seats in the House of Lords.

In most though not all dioceses, the diocesan bishop has the assistance of one or more suffragan bishops. Every suffragan bishop, on his appointment, is accorded a titular see, which is invariably, in practice, named after some place within the diocese.

A suffragan bishop is, in law, appointed for the diocese as a whole, and not to any particular area within the diocese. But under the Dioceses Measure 1978, s. 10, a diocesan bishop has power to make a temporary delegation to a suffragan bishop of any of his functions within a specified area. And s. 11 of the Measure contains provisions under which a reorganisation or other scheme, made according to the procedure laid down by the Measure, may provide for the division of a diocese into areas (called 'episcopal areas') and for specifying the bishop (being either the diocesan or a suffragan bishop) or bishops (being the diocesan bishop and a suffragan bishop) who are to have or share the episcopal oversight of each area. But the making of any such scheme is not to be taken as divesting the diocesan bishop of any of his functions (which will accordingly continue to be exercisable by him at his discretion throughout the diocese).[1]

Dioceses are divided into archdeaconries, which in turn consist of rural deaneries. These units are interposed between the parish and the diocese for certain purposes, although the two latter are the only units necessary to a parochial system. It follows that as a general rule each parish is in (1) a rural deanery, (2) an archdeaconry, (3) a diocese, and (4) a province. The two latter have been briefly described.

(3) THE ARCHDEACONRY

An archdeaconry may extend to the whole of a diocese, but is usually smaller. At its head is the archdeacon, who on appointment must have completed at least six years in priest's orders. He is usually (though not always) appointed by the bishop, and before entering upon his office subscribes the declaration of assent set out in Canon C15,[2] and takes the oath of allegiance. An archdeacon is entitled by custom to the style of address 'The Venerable'.

Subject to the paramount rights of the bishop of the diocese, an archdeacon has the power of visitation within his archdeaconry, and it is at his visitation after the end of

[1] The Diocese of London has, in accordance with these provisions, been divided by scheme into five episcopal areas; but no scheme for division into areas has as yet been made in respect of any other diocese.

[2] As to the nature of this declaration, see p. 33 *post*.

April (when the bishop does not hold one) that churchwardens are admitted to office.

In addition, powers are conferred on the archdeacon for the enforcement of the provisions for the quinquennial inspection of churches contained in the Inspection of Churches Measure 1955. He also 'inducts' clergy who are presented to benefices, i.e. places them in possession of the *temporalities* of the benefice.

The archdeacon is a member of the Diocesan Board of Patronage when that board is transacting any business relating to a benefice in his archdeaconry.

One of the archdeacons in every diocese is a member of the Lower House of Convocation, and of the House of Clergy of the General Synod.

(4) THE RURAL DEANERY

The rural deanery is a collection of parishes for administrative purposes with an archdeaconry. Its significance as an ecclesiastical unit has been enhanced as a result of the creation, by the Synodical Government Measure 1969, of deanery synods, in which important functions are vested.[1]

Each rural deanery is presided over by a rural dean who is usually (though not necessarily) one of the beneficed clergy in the deanery. He is the bishop's officer and may be removed from office at any time.

Apart from this and a few other statutory functions, his duties are such (e.g. of inquiry and report about specific matters) as may from time to time be deputed to him by the bishop or archdeacon. According to some authorities he may, in the absence of the archdeacon, 'induct' to a benefice: but it is doubtful whether he is qualified to do this except as the archdeacon's deputy.

[1] See p. 8 *post*.

The rural dean is a member of the Diocesan Board of Patronage when that Board is transacting any business relating to a benefice in his deanery. He, and an elected member of the house of laity of the deanery synod, are joint chairmen of that synod.

(5) SYNODICAL GOVERNMENT

(a) *Historical Background*

Down to the year 1919, the Sovereign in Parliament was the only institution having unlimited power to legislate for the affairs of the Church of England. An Act of Parliament could (as it still can) effect any alteration whatever in the law of the Church.

A subsidiary legislative power was vested in the two Convocations of Canterbury and York, bodies composed entirely of bishops and clergy which, after a long lapse, had been revived in 1852 and 1861 respectively. Each Convocation had power to legislate by passing canons, but it was a strictly conditional and limited power. In the first place a canon, to be effective at all, required the royal assent; secondly, it was only effective within the province whose Convocation passed it; thirdly, it was ineffective in so far as it conflicted with existing common law or statute; and finally, a canon was directly binding only on the clergy and holders of ecclesiastical offices (such as churchwardens) but not on the laity generally.

The Church of England Assembly (Powers) Act 1919 gave legal authority to the body called 'The National Assembly of the Church of England' ('The Church Assembly' for short) in which was vested a general power, subject to the control of Parliament, to legislate upon matters concerning the Church of England.

Stated very shortly, the general scheme of the Act was as follows. The Church Assembly, as constituted by the Act, consisted of three Houses; the House of Bishops, the House of Clergy (both derived from the Convocations), and the House of Laity. Power was conferred on the Assembly to propose and pass new laws called 'Measures'. Any measure, having been passed in the Assembly and having been (in effect) endorsed by resolution of both Houses of Parliament, and having received the royal assent, was given the same force and effect as an Act of Parliament.

The Synodical Government Measure 1969, whilst building on the scheme of Church government established in 1919 and subsequent years, introduced such considerable alterations and reforms that it created a more or less entirely new system. Under the scheme introduced by the Measure, 'synods', each of them with a mixed clerical and lay membership, were established at the national, diocesan and ruri-decanal levels; such synods being known as the 'General Synod', 'diocesan synods' and 'deanery synods' respectively.

(b) *The General Synod*

The General Synod, though continuous in identity with the former Church Assembly, was largely re-constituted, and it inherited not only the power of the Church Assembly to legislate by measure, but also the former power of the Convocations to make canons (which power was transferred to it from the Convocations). It is also empowered to pass subordinate legislation, and to make regulations (known as 'Acts of Synod') in cases where a measure or canon would be inappropriate. Apart from its legislative powers, the General Synod conducts debates upon matters of religious or public interest.

(c) *Diocesan Synods*

A diocesan synod is composed of three houses viz. a house of bishops, a house of clergy and a house of laity. Its functions are to consider matters concerning the Church of England and to make provision for such matters in relation to the diocese; to consider and express an opinion on other matters of religious or public interest; to advise the bishop on any matters on which he may consult the synod; and to consider and express an opinion on any matters referred to it by the General Synod.

It is the duty of the bishop to consult with the diocesan synod on matters of general concern and importance to the diocese.

The diocesan synod is enjoined to keep the deanery synods of the diocese informed of the policies and problems of the diocese and of the business which is to come before meetings of the diocesan synod, and it may delegate executive functions to deanery synods. It is also enjoined to keep itself informed, through the deanery synods, of events and opinions in the parishes, and to give opportunities at its meetings for discussing matters raised by deanery synods and parochial church councils.

(d) *Deanery Synods*

A deanery synod consists of a house of clergy and a house of laity. It exercises at deanery level deliberative powers similar to those of the diocesan synod, as well as bringing together the views of the parishes in the deanery on common problems, making known provisions made by the diocesan synod, considering the business of the diocesan synod, and raising such matters with it as the deanery synod considers appropriate.

Deanery synods are enjoined to exercise any functions which may be delegated to them by the diocesan synod in relation to the parishes of their deaneries, and in particular (if so delegated) the determination of parochial shares in 'quotas' allocated to the deaneries (meaning the amount to be subscribed to the expenditure authorised by the diocesan synod).

2

The Courts of the Church

(1) Diocesan Courts—(2) Provincial Courts—(3) Court of Ecclesiastical Causes Reserved—(4) Proceedings for Ecclesiastical Offences.

(1) DIOCESAN COURTS

The law relating to ecclesiastical courts and the trial of ecclesiastical cases was much revised, and to a large extent codified, by the Ecclesiastical Jurisdiction Measure 1963.

Under that Measure (as previously), every archbishop (in his diocesan capacity) and every diocesan bishop has a court for the trial of ecclesiastical matters arising in his diocese. In the Diocese of Canterbury this court is known as the Commissary Court and elsewhere as the Consistory Court. The judge of the court is, in Canterbury, styled the 'Commissary General' and in other dioceses the 'Chancellor'. In this book, the expressions 'consistory court' and 'chancellor' are intended to cover the diocesan court and its judge in every diocese including Canterbury.

The chancellor is appointed by the bishop. He must be at least thirty years old and either a barrister of seven years' standing or a person who has held high judicial office; and if the bishop appoints a layman, he must satisfy himself that the appointee is a communicant. If the chancellor's appointment is confirmed by the dean and chapter or the cathedral chapter of the cathedral church (as in practice it usually is)[1], he remains in office until death or resignation, subject (in the case of a chancellor appointed on or after the 1st March 1965) to a power for the bishop to remove him if the Upper House of the Convocation of the province resolves that he is incapable of acting or unfit to act; and subject also (in the case of a chancellor appointed on or after the 25th April 1976) to compulsory retirement at the age of 75.

The status of the bishop in his own court depends upon the terms of the patent appointing the chancellor. In some cases the bishop expressly reserves to himself the power to sit and try certain cases or classes of cases.[2] But except so far as this power is reserved, the chancellor is the sole judge, and indeed may try cases to which the bishop himself is a party.

The consistory court is the court of first instance for the trial of faculty cases (as to which see the next chapter), and also for the trial of proceedings against priests or deacons for offences not involving any matter of doctrine, ritual or ceremonial.

(2) PROVINCIAL COURTS

The provincial courts of Canterbury and York are known respectively as the Court of Arches (or Arches Court of Canterbury) and the Chancery Court of York.

There are five judges of each court. One of them, who is a judge of both courts, is appointed by the two archbishops subject to the approval of the Queen: in the Province of Canterbury he is styled 'Dean of the Arches', and in that of York 'Auditor'. Of the other four judges in each court, two are clergymen appointed by the prolocutor of the Lower House of Convocation of the relevant province; and two

[1] The appointment of a chancellor which is not so confirmed determines on a new bishop taking office, though he may be reappointed.

[2] This applies only to the Faculty Jurisdiction (see pp. 15 and 16 *post*) and not to the Criminal Jurisdiction.

are communicant laymen possessing judicial experience, appointed by the Chairman of the House of Laity of the General Synod after consultation with the Lord Chancellor.

Each provincial court is the court of appeal from the consistory courts within the province in faculty cases not involving matters of doctrine, ritual or ceremonial (for the hearing of which cases the Dean of the Arches or Auditor sits alone); also in proceedings against priests and deacons for offences not involving such matters (for the hearing of which all five judges sit).

In faculty cases there is a further appeal from the provincial court to the Judicial Committee of the Privy Council.

(3) COURT OF ECCLESIASTICAL CAUSES RESERVED

This court consists of five judges appointed by the Queen. Two of them are persons who hold or have held high judicial office and who are communicants, and the other three are persons who are, or have been, diocesan bishops.

This court is the court of first instance for proceedings against the clergy for offences against the laws ecclesiastical involving matters of doctrine, ritual or ceremonial. It is also the court of appeal from consistory courts in faculty cases involving such matters. In either class of case, there is a final appeal from the Court of Ecclesiastical Causes Reserved to a 'Commission of Review', consisting of three lay Lords of Appeal who are communicants, and two diocesan bishops who are members of the House of Lords.

(4) PROCEEDINGS FOR ECCLESIASTICAL OFFENCES

There are special provisions in the Measure of 1963 (as amended by the Ecclesiastical Jurisdiction (Amendment) Measure 1974) as regards the trial of archbishops and bishops for ecclesiastical offences, but space does not permit their detailed consideration.[1] Something, however, should be said of the nature of proceedings against priests and deacons.

All such proceedings commence with a complaint laid before the registrar of the diocese. Any person authorised by the bishop may lay a complaint. A complaint may also be laid, in the case of an incumbent or of a stipendiary curate (i.e. a priest-in-charge or assistant curate), or of a curate-in-charge of a conventional district, by six or more persons of full age whose names are on the electoral roll; or, in the case of an assistant curate, by his incumbent.

The procedure following upon a complaint differs according as to whether any matter of doctrine, ritual or ceremonial is involved. If no such matter is involved, the bishop, after giving both the accused and the complainant the opportunity of a private interview, may decide either to take no further steps (and thereby to put an end to the proceedings) or to refer the matter to an 'examiner', who is selected for the purpose from a panel of examiners consisting of qualified lawyers. It is the function of the examiner to inquire into the complaint and to decide whether there is a case for the accused to answer. If he decides that there is no such case, that ends the proceedings. But if he decides that there is such a case, he must specify the alleged offence in his report, and the next step is for the bishop to nominate a fit person to promote a complaint against the accused in the consistory court. At the hearing in that court, the chancellor (or a duly qualified person appointed by him with the bishop's consent to take his place) sits as judge, with four assessors (two clerical and two lay) appointed from a panel of assessors to act as jury. If as a result of the trial the accused is found guilty, he is sentenced by the chancellor,

[1] It should be noted that these special provisions will apply to any consecrated bishop, even though the office (if any) for the time being held by him is not in its nature episcopal (e.g. he is an incumbent of a parish).

who may pronounce on the accused such of the censures mentioned below as he thinks fit.

A priest or deacon may be put on trial under the procedure outlined above for any ecclesiastical offence not involving doctrine, ritual or ceremonial, including in particular (i) conduct unbecoming the office and work of a clerk in holy orders, and (ii) serious, persistent, or continuous neglect of duty.

At any time after the laying of the original complaint, the bishop, after consulting the complainant and with the consent of the accused, may pronounce a censure forthwith, and the proceedings are then at an end. In effect, the accused's consent is treated as a plea of guilty.

Any of the following censures can be pronounced by the chancellor after a trial or by the bishop if the accused has consented to summary disposal by the bishop, viz. deprivation from existing preferment, coupled with disqualification from future preferment except on certain conditions; inhibition, i.e. disqualification for a specified period from exercising the functions of his order; suspension from his preferment for a specified period; monition, i.e. an order to do or refrain from doing a specified act; or rebuke. If a sentence of deprivation is pronounced by either the chancellor after trial or by the bishop on summary disposal, the bishop may also (subject to a right for the accused to appeal to the archbishop)[1] depose the accused from holy orders, and any such deposition can subsequently be reversed only by a free pardon from the Crown.

There are provisions in the Measure of 1963 (as amended) for the pronouncement of censure of deprivation on a priest or deacon as a result of any of certain findings against him in a secular court, without any further trial in a church court.

If a complaint against a priest or deacon involves a

[1] If the decision is an archbishop's, the appeal lies to the other archbishop.

matter of doctrine, ritual or ceremonial, the bishop, after giving both the accused and the complainant an opportunity of being interviewed in private, must decide either that no further step is to be taken, or to refer the complaint to a specially constituted committee for inquiry. Such committee consists of one member of the Upper House and two members of the Lower House of the Convocation of the province, and two chancellors of dioceses in the province. No further steps are to be taken in the matter if the committee, after due inquiry, decides that there is no case for the accused to answer, or alternatively that, although there is a case for him to answer, the offence is too trivial to warrant further proceedings, or that there were extenuating circumstances, or that further proceedings would not be in the interests of the Church. If, however, the committee recommends further proceedings, the Upper House of Convocation has to nominate a fit person to promote a complaint against the accused in the Court of Ecclesiastical Causes Reserved, and the case is brought before that court accordingly. There is provision whereby the court, in the trial of any case, will have the assistance of three to five expert advisers. If the court finds the accused guilty, it decides on and pronounces the appropriate censure; but no censure more severe than monition can be pronounced in the case of a first offence.

All decisions in the Court of Ecclesiastical Causes Reserved are by a majority of the judges.

3

Faculties

The consecrated buildings and lands situated within a diocese are in the ultimate guardianship of the bishop, who exercises his authority in this respect through his chancellor. In consequence the legal proceeding known as the application for and the granting of a faculty is necessary for the sanction of alterations in a consecrated building or its contents, or in a churchyard or other consecrated burial ground or its contents.

The faculty jurisdiction extends to unconsecrated land which forms, or is part of, the curtilage of a consecrated church (Faculty Jurisdiction Measure 1964, section 7). And it may also be extended, by an order of the bishop, and during the period specified in such order, to any unconsecrated building which he has licensed for public worship (section 6).

The petition for a faculty is lodged in the consistory court of the diocese, before the chancellor as judge of that court. It is usually made in the name of the incumbent and churchwardens, but this is not necessary, since any person who is regarded by the law as having an interest is entitled either to apply for or to oppose the grant of a faculty; and for this purpose all the following persons are regarded as having an interest, viz. the parishioners, persons who though not resident in the parish are on its electrocal roll, and the archdeacon;[1] and also in some types of case, certain other persons as well.

The object of obtaining a faculty is to ensure that the work proposed to be done shall not subsequently be interfered with, for if anything is done without the grant of a faculty, it is open to any parishioner, or other person having an interest, to apply for a faculty authorising the removal of the work. In such a case the incumbent and churchwardens, or any other person or persons also having an interest, may lodge a cross-petition for a confirmatory faculty authorising retrospectively what is sought to be removed.

Trivial additions to the church or its furniture, e.g. alms-boxes or hassocks, do not require a faculty.

As regards the churchyard, no faculty is necessary for the burial of a body; on the other hand, a body cannot be removed from consecrated ground for burial elsewhere without a faculty. For the erection of a monument, a faculty is required in strict law, but usually this is not insisted on in practice, and the incumbent's approval is regarded as sufficient. If he refuses approval, the person desirous of erecting the monument can petition for a faculty to reverse his decision.[2]

Trivial repairs or replacements do not require a faculty. But the decision whether a faculty is necessary in any given case rests with the chancellor, and it is desirable that any question of doubt should be referred to him.

[1] See Faculty Jurisdiction Measure 1964, section 2. If the archdeaconry is vacant, or if the archdeacon is incapacitated or unable or unwilling to act, the bishop may appoint another person to act in his place.

[2] In many dioceses the chancellor has issued a Directive indicating the nature of the monuments (size and type of stone) which are usually considered suitable for that locality and has indicated that, within the terms of the Directive, he is content for the incumbent to permit their introduction without the need for a faculty. The legal effect of such a Directive is open to doubt; but in practice such schemes work well, and, since the jurisdiction of the consistory court cannot be ousted, it is open to any interested party to have recourse to the court.

No faculty may be granted for anything illegal, e.g. because it has a superstitious purpose, or because it would be inconsistent with the sacred purposes for which the building or land is consecrated. But within the limits of legality, the consistory court has an extremely wide discretion to give or refuse a faculty for almost any sort of work or innovation. This discretion must, however, be exercised judicially and for proper reasons. Certain conditions and restrictions are imposed by the Faculty Jurisdiction Measure 1964 on the grant of a faculty for the demolition or partial demolition of a church.

The jurisdiction of the consistory court extends only to those places where the bishop is the ordinary[1]. He is the ordinary for most of the geographical area covered by the diocese, but not for places known as peculiars, for example, Westminster Abbey, nor usually (and perhaps surprisingly) for his cathedral church where in most cases the dean (or provost) is the ordinary and sometimes the dean (or provost) and chapter fulfil that role. With such places, usually non-parochial, this book is not concerned.

There is in every diocese an Advisory Committee whose function it is to assist the chancellor on the one hand and the parishioners on the other. These committees usually consist of experts in architecture, archaeology, and art, who know the diocese and its churches. They are ready to advise the parishioners before the proposals are embodied in a petition for a faculty, and the chancellor on any proposals submitted to him. The advisory committee system has justified itself by results, and considerable attention is given to the committees by most chancellors. A Central Council for the Care of Churches also exists, the purpose of which is to co-ordinate the work of the diocesan committees and to advise in cases which present special difficulty.

In a simple case, where there is no opposition, a chancellor may, and commonly does, grant a faculty without a

[1] See p. 2 *ante*.

hearing in court. But if in his opinion the case involves some legal or other difficulty or complication, he is likely to direct a hearing in open court; and he will always do so if the petition is opposed.

Under the Faculty Jurisdiction Measure 1964, section 12, the archdeacon is empowered to issue a certificate for certain types of work which will take effect in lieu of a faculty, provided that application is made to him by the incumbent and churchwardens of the parish, and is supported by a resolution of the parochial church council, and is unopposed. The works in question are:

(a) Repairs to a church not involving substantial change in its structure nor affecting its appearance;
(b) Repairs to the contents of a church not materially affecting their nature or appearance;
(c) Redecoration of a church or its contents;
(d) Any alteration in an existing heating system not involving a substantial change in the church's appearance.

The chancellor may direct the same procedure with regard to any other application which, in his opinion, is unlikely to give rise to any controversy or dissatisfaction in the parish and is not important enough to justify the expense of faculty proceedings.

4

The Parish

(1) Ancient Parishes—(2) New and Altered Parishes—(3) Unions of Beneficies and Parishes—(4) Team and Group Ministries—(5) Conventional Districts—(6) Sharing of Church Buildings—(7) Guild Churches.

(1) ANCIENT PARISHES

A parish is an area committed to the incumbent by the bishop for the cure (i.e. care) of souls. Within the parish the incumbent is, under the bishop, supreme, but his supremacy is constitutional and not arbitrary. He is the bishop's deputy for most purposes within the parish, and his 'cure' is exercised to the exclusion of other clergy.[1]

The growth of the parochial system was a gradual process. While the bishop is the incumbent, and the cathedral

[1] This exclusive right of the incumbent is modified by the Extra-Parochial Ministry Measure 1967, which entitles a minister of any parish to perform offices and services at the home of a person who is on the electoral roll of his parish but resident in another parish, without the consent and free from the control of the minister of that other parish; and which also empowers the bishop of a diocese to license a clergyman to officiate within the diocese in the premises of any university, college, school, hospital, or public or charitable institution, without the consent and free from the control of the minister of the parish in which the premises are situated.

is the parish church, of the whole diocese, and the only essential 'parson' for the existence of a diocese is the bishop with his cathedral church, it became necessary at an early stage for him to have assistants in his ministrations. It may be mentioned that the term 'parson' is really a corrupt abbreviation of *ecclesiae persona* or 'ecclesiastical person'. The first stage of parochial development was for the bishop to ordain clergy to assist him in the diocese, who were then sent out by him to preach and administer the sacraments in any district to which he might assign them. As yet no churches existed, and the clergy resided with the bishop where his *cathedra* or 'seat' was.

In course of time, churches were built and endowed, and they required clergy to minister in them. The person who built the church usually nominated a layman for ordination to the cure, or a priest to perform the duties there. Very often the founder of the church would be the local lord of the manor. In this growth of church buildings we see the beginnings of the right to present clergy to incumbencies, a right vested in some person, not necessarily the bishop, which is familiar at the present day. The person in whom the right is vested is now known as the 'patron', and his status is historically derived from the 'lord' who built a church on his demesne, and nominated the man of his choice as the minister of that church. The country gradually became covered with churches, each of which served a district which coincided more or less with a political area, and these districts are the predecessors of the parishes of modern times.

While this was the normal process, it sometimes happened that the bishop would assign a district to a church, and place one of his clergy there.

But, however the local conditions varied, the priest who served each church was called 'curate', as a person to whom the cure of souls was delegated. The districts assigned to churches came to be called parishes; and by the end of the thirteenth century practically the whole realm had been divided up into parishes, and the ecclesiastical units so formed are now termed '*ancient* parishes'.

(2) NEW AND ALTERED PARISHES

As was to be expected, changed circumstances, especially increases in the population of urban and suburban areas, demanded modifications in the scheme of ancient parishes. From the early nineteenth century onwards, a number of Acts of Parliament, notably the Church Building Acts 1818 to 1884 and the New Parishes Acts 1843 to 1884, were passed to enable new parishes or districts to be created where they were required. For all practical purposes, all these Acts were repealed and replaced by the New Parishes Measure 1943, the relevant provisions of which have now themselves been repealed, and replaced successively by the Pastoral Measure 1968 and the Pastoral Measure 1983.

Numerous parishes have been created over the years under these various statutes and are now in existence. Although they are in fact modern ecclesiastical units, the law relating to them is, for practical purposes, virtually the same as the law relating to ancient parishes.

The only statutory provisions now in force for the creation of new parishes, or the alteration of existing ones, are those contained in the Pastoral Measure 1983 itself. This Measure provides for the establishment in every diocese of a Pastoral Committee, and for the making by the Church Commissioners of 'pastoral schemes', based on proposals submitted by the Pastoral Committee with the approval of the bishop; any such scheme takes effect on its being confirmed by Order in Council. At various stages in the proceedings leading to the making and confirmation of a scheme, there are provisions for ascertaining the views of 'interested parties' (who include, amongst others, all incumbents, patrons and parochial church councils liable to be concerned); for giving notice, both in the press and to particular persons, of the objects of the intended scheme and of its submission for confirmation; and for dealing with any written representations which may be received with respect to it. Any person who has made written representations with respect to a scheme, and whose objections have not been met, may apply for leave to appeal to the Judicial Committee of the Privy Council; and the scheme will not be confirmed until the appeal has been decided.

Amongst the matters for which a pastoral scheme may provide are the following, viz.: the creation, by union or otherwise, of new benefices[1] or parishes; the dissolution of existing benefices or parishes; and the alteration of the areas of existing benefices or parishes (including the transfer of a parish from one benefice to another) or the definition of their boundaries.

There are wide powers in the Measure for enabling a scheme to deal with churches in the area to which it extends. If the scheme makes no provision with respect to the churches in the affected area, they simply retain their pre-existing status. Any church in the new or altered parish may, however, be designated as the parish church or as an additional parish church, and the Measure enables there to be more than one parish church or additional church within the parish. A new church provided under a scheme may become the parish church or an additional parish church once it has been approved by the Church Commissioners and consecrated.

A scheme may create a new parish with full parochial status although there will be no parish church when the scheme comes into operation. In such a case, and in any other case of a parish having no parish church, as soon as a church within the parish is approved by the Church Commissioners and is consecrated, it becomes the parish church. Meanwhile, the bishop is enjoined to license one or more buildings or parts of buildings for public worship; he may also designate any building or part of a building so

[1] As to the meaning of 'benefice', see p. 23 *post*.

licensed as the 'parish centre of worship', whereupon, so long as the designation remains in force, it is deemed to be the parish church for all legal purposes, including the solemnisation of marriages. (This does not affect the right, under the Marriage Act 1949, of parishioners intending to be married to resort for the purpose to the church of an adjoining parish until their own parish has an actual parish church. Meanwhile, they have an option in the matter.)

Any church in an area affected by a scheme which is deprived by the scheme of the status of a parish church, or which does not acquire that status under the scheme, will either continue in use as a chapel-of-ease, or be declared redundant by the scheme. The Measure lays down a complicated procedure for dealing with redundant churches which it is beyond the scope of this book to describe in detail. As a rule, unless there is some suitable use to which a redundant church can be put or for which it can be disposed of by sale or otherwise, it is liable eventually to be demolished; but there are special provisions concerning the preservation of churches of historical or architectural interest.

Some of the powers conferred by the Measure may be exercised by a 'pastoral order' instead of by a pastoral scheme. The procedure for making an order is relatively simple: the order is proposed by the Church Commissioners and made by the bishop; no confirmation by Order in Council is necessary, and there is no appeal to the Judicial Committee of the Privy Council. But any proposals for the creation or dissolution or union of benefices or parishes, or for transferring any church used for public worship from any benefice or parish, or for making any church redundant, can only be given effect to by a scheme.

(3) UNIONS OF BENEFICES AND PARISHES

Within the context of the parochial ministry, a benefice may be defined as the office of the rector or vicar (i.e. of the incumbent) of a parish. Thus a union of benefices, without more, entails simply the concentration of both or all of the incumbencies of two or more parishes, as one office or benefice, in the hands of one incumbent. The identity of the parishes themselves is not affected; each of them remains a separate parish, with its own parish church and parochial organisation. The only essential legal link between them is that their combined incumbencies have become a single office, held by a single incumbent whom they share.

A union of parishes necessarily involves a union of the benefices of the parishes concerned. But it also entails the loss, by each of those parishes, of its separate identity, and the merger of both or all of them into a single new united parish.

The Pastoral Measure 1968 repealed and superseded all the earlier legislation relating to unions; and any proposed union of benefices or parishes can now only be effected by a pastoral scheme under the provisions outlined above. The Measure of 1983 contains full powers for the purpose, and in particular declares that a pastoral scheme providing for the union of two or more benefices may provide for uniting all the parishes within the area of the new benefice, or for uniting some but not all of them, or may leave them as separate parishes.

(4) TEAM AND GROUP MINISTRIES

In recent years, in various parts of the country, there have been experiments based on the idea of an association of clergymen co-operating in the running of an area considerably larger than a normal parish.

In different places there may be different reasons for such an experiment. In some areas (mostly rural) it can be an effective method of coping with a shortage of clergy, by deploying the available clergy to the best advantage. Elsewhere, in thickly populated built-up areas (such as a 'new town' or a suburb of recent growth) a considerable modification of the ordinary parochial system may be thought desirable, on account of the difficulty of dividing an area of this sort into parishes of normal size, each capable of existing as a separate community with a life of its own. Yet another possible advantage of these arrangements is the scope and opportunity they can offer to clergy with specialist training or talents.

The Pastoral Measure 1983 affords a legal basis for team and group ministries, by enacting that a pastoral scheme may provide for the establishment of a ministry of either of these two sorts. It also contains provisions defining and safeguarding the status of the clergy engaged in them.

A team ministry is a ministry which normally covers the area of a single benefice, although it may be extended to the area of two or more benefices if and so long as all such benefices are held in plurality by the same incumbent. Any benefice concerned may of course, as a result of a union of benefices, contain any number of separate parishes. Under the provisions of the Measure, the incumbent of the benefice or benefices is styled 'rector', and is the principal member of the team. The other clergy in the team are styled 'vicars'.

A group ministry is a ministry covering two or more benefices with different incumbents, the general principle being that each incumbent will, besides attending to his own benefice, assist the incumbents of the other benefices.

Either a team or a group ministry may be dissolved by a subsequent pastoral scheme.

Broadly, the contrast between a team ministry and a group ministry is that the former operates on the basis of a team under a leader (the incumbent or 'rector'), whilst the latter is a partnership of equals, each of whom is an incumbent with primacy in the area of his own benefice.

Both types of ministry are primarily concerned with the organisation of clerical man-power within a particular area; and the status and duties of the participating clergy will be more particularly considered in the next chapter. But in relation to both of them, the Measure also contains special provisions as regards such matters as patronage and parochial church councils, and these provisions will be noted, later in this book, under the appropriate heads.

(5) CONVENTIONAL DISTRICTS

Conventional districts are sometimes formed in anticipation of their subsequently becoming distinct parishes; they are unaffected by the Pastoral Measure 1983. They are not parishes, but merely areas which are placed, with the consent of the incumbent and the bishop, under the care of a 'curate-in-charge' upon whom devolves the responsibility for the cure of souls in the district. The arrangement requires renewal with every change in the incumbency of the parish in which the district lies.

So long as a conventional district exists, it has an organisation similar to that of a parish. In particular, it has its own churchwardens, electoral roll and parochial church council.

Conventional districts are now the only sort of 'ecclesiastical districts' capable of existing in law. The Pastoral Measure 1968 converted all other districts then existing into parishes, and abolished the machinery for creating new ones.

(6) SHARING OF CHURCH BUILDINGS

The Sharing of Church Buildings Act 1969 was passed with the general object of facilitating agreements (termed 'sharing agreements') for the sharing and use of church buildings by different Christian bodies. Where a parish or other church of the Church of England is the subject-matter of a sharing agreement, or where the competent authorities of the Church of England enter into a sharing agreement in relation to a church belonging to some other

Christian body, or to a church proposed to be built, this is likely to have a considerable effect on the life and organisation of the parish concerned.[1]

The Churches which may be parties to a sharing agreement include the Church of England, the Roman Catholic Church, and all the principal Free Church bodies. Any two or more of such Churches may enter into a sharing agreement with respect to any existing or proposed church building or buildings. In the case of the Church of England, the Diocesan Board of Finance of the diocese concerned, and the incumbent and parochial church council of the parish concerned, are necessary parties to any sharing agreement; and the consent of the bishop and the Pastoral Committee of the diocese must also be obtained. The necesary parties to a sharing agreement on behalf of the Roman Catholic Church or any Free Church are such persons as may be determined by the appropriate authority of that Church.

As regards ownership, a sharing agreement may provide for the shared buildings or building to be owned by one only of the sharing Churches or to be jointly owned by all or some of them. But this is subject to the qualification that no existing consecrated church of the Church of England must remain in the sole ownership of the Church of England, unless authority is given by a pastoral scheme to provide for joint ownership by the Church of England and another Church or Churches. An unconsecrated church building which is the subject-matter of a sharing agreement is not permitted to be consecrated, unless under the agreement it is in the sole ownership of the Church of England. And any church building which is shared by the Church of England under a sharing agreement may only become or

[1] Although the statements in the text are primarily concerned with the sharing of places of worship, it should be mentioned that sharing agreements can also be made under the Act with respect to church buildings of certain other types: viz. parish halls, youth clubs or centres, and places of residence for ministers or lay workers.

remain a parish church if, under the agreement, it is in the sole ownership of the Church of England; but even if it is not in such sole ownership, its designation as a 'parish centre of worship'[1] is permissible.

A sharing agreement must make provision (amongst other things) for determining the extent to which any church building to which it applies is to be available for worship in accordance with the forms and practice of the sharing Churches; and for dealing with financial obligations as to repairs, furnishings, etc. It must also contain appropriate provisions for its own termination.

(7) GUILD CHURCHES

The status of 'guild churches' is peculiar to the City of London, and is the creation of the City of London (Guild Churches) Act 1952 (a private Act). Although guild churches are not parish churches, the Act gives them a comparable organisation and it is convenient to mention them briefly here.

The status was devised as a method of dealing with the special circumstances obtaining in the City, where on the one hand there are far more churches than are necessary for the needs of resident Sunday worshippers; but on the other hand, there is on working days a vast influx of non-residents who are proper objects of pastoral care, and many of whom are attendants at week-day services in City churches.

A number of former parish churches in the City have been converted into guild churches under the Act of 1952, or the City of London (Guild Churches) Act 1960 (which amended it in certain respects). As such, they no longer have the status of parish churches; nevertheless, they are wholly independent of the parishes in which they are respectively situated. Each guild church has a minister, who

[1] See p. 23 *ante*.

is appointed by a patron, is licensed by the bishop, is free from any control by the incumbent of the parish, and is entitled to the style of 'vicar'. His period of office, initially five years, may be extended from time to time for additional periods of three years each. In relation to the guild church and its churchyard he has the same rights and duties as those of a parish incumbent in relation to the parish church and churchyard; but he is under no liability to provide Sunday services. An assistant curate may also be appointed.

As from the 1st January 1976, under the Ecclesiastical Offices (Age Limit) Measure 1975, no clergyman aged 70 or over may be appointed vicar of a guild church, and any vicar of a guild church appointed on or after that date is subject to provisions for compulsory retirement at the age of 70 or upwards similar to those affecting an incumbent (see p. 43 *post*).

Provision is made by the Act of 1952 for churchwardens and sidesmen of a guild church, for a guild church electoral roll, and for a guild church council, which is analogous to a parochial church council and similarly composed.

5

The Parochial Clergy

(1) The Incumbent; (*a*) Rectors and Vicars; (*b*) Institution and Collation; (*c*) Induction; (*d*) Conduct of Services; (*e*) Incumbent's other Duties; (*f*) Enforcement of Duties; (*g*) Avoidance of Benefice; (*h*) Sequestrations—(2) The Unbeneficed Clergy; (*a*) Generally; (*b*) Priests-in-Charge; (*c*) Assistant Curates—(3) Members of Team and Group Ministries.

(1) THE INCUMBENT

(a) *Rectors and Vicars*

The smallest normal unit of organisation is, as has been already indicated, the parish, at the head of which is the incumbent, who has the cure of souls therein, and is either a 'rector' or a 'vicar'. The difference between a rector and a vicar is historical rather than practical. Briefly, it may be said that where the whole of the tithe and glebe were attached to the benefice for the maintenance of the minister, that benefice is a rectory. Where there is a mere vicarage, a monastery formerly had the rights of the rector, and took the glebe and tithe whilst providing a vicar to attend to the parochial duties. At the dissolution of the monasteries, laymen became rectors in place of the monasteries and took the tithe.

Previously to the Pastoral Measure 1968, there was a third class of benefice called a perpetual curacy, which arose where the incumbent was neither a rector, nor was an endowment provided out of the income of the rectory for his maintenance; the benefices of new ecclesiastical parishes were as a rule perpetual curacies. But the Measure converted all perpetual curacies into vicarages. The incumbencies of districts converted by the same Measure into parishes are likewise vicarages.

On a union, by a pastoral scheme, of two or more benefices one of which is a rectory, the new benefice created by the union is a rectory. And on the dissolution of a rectory under a pastoral scheme, otherwise than as a result of a union of benefices, the benefice in the area of which the residence of the rector of the dissolved benefice is situated is likewise a rectory. But except in those two cases, or in the case of a team ministry, every new benefice created by a pastoral scheme is a vicarage.

In the context of team ministries, the expressions 'rector' and 'vicar' have special meanings which are considered later in this chapter.

(b) *Institution and Collation*

An incumbent is 'presented' to the bishop by the patron of the benefice, except where the bishop himself is the patron. He is put in possession of the cure of souls by the bishop by a process known as institution, or, where the bishop is patron, as collation.[1]

[1] As to the considerable alterations in the law relating to patronage, and to rights of presentation or collation, which are contained in the Patronage (Benefices) Measure 1986, see Chapter 6 *post*, particularly pp. 57 to 58k.

Under the Benefices Act 1898, the bishop can refuse to institute a presentee if, at the date of the vacancy, not more than one year has elapsed since a transfer of the advowson (unless it be proved that the transfer was not effected in view of the probability of a vacancy within the year); or on the ground that at the date of presentation not more than three years have elapsed since the presentee was made a deacon; or on the ground of the unfitness of the presentee by reason of physical or mental infirmity or incapacity, or serious pecuniary embarrassment, or for any of the moral reasons specified in the Act; or on the ground of his having, with reference to the presentation, been knowingly party or privy to any transaction or agreement which is invalid under the Act.

Under the Benefices Measure 1972, the bishop may also refuse to institute on the ground that the presentee (not having previously held a benefice or been a vicar in a team ministry) has had less than three years' experience as a full-time parochial minister.

If the bishop refuses to institute on any of these grounds, the patron or the presentee has a right of appeal to a special court constituted by the Act of 1898.

As from the 1st January 1976, by virtue of the Ecclesiastical Offices (Age Limit) Measure 1975, no clergyman aged 70 or over may be presented or collated to a benefice.[1]

Before the incumbent is instituted, the notice of the bishop's intention to admit[2] must be sent to the churchwardens and affixed by them to the church door, where it must remain for a calendar month, and the presentee must

[1] An exception is made by the Church of England (Miscellaneous Provisions) Measure 1978, s. 2, by virtue of which the Measure of 1975 is not to be taken as invalidating any provision in a pastoral scheme or order for designating a person over the age of 70 as the holder of an office, if immediately before the scheme or order came into operation, and also on the 1st January 1976, he was the incumbent of a benefice affected by the scheme or order.

[2] See p. 74 *post.*

subscribe the declaration of assent,[1] and take the oaths of allegiance[2] and of canonical obedience. These preliminaries are also necessary before collation.

(c) *Induction*

The incumbent is put into possession of the temporalities of the benefice by the process known as 'induction', which is performed by the archdeacon on the mandate of the bishop. Induction is sometimes performed by the rural dean, but it is doubtful whether he can act except as the archdeacon's deputy and on his mandate. In practice, institution and induction take place usually at a service held at the parish church, but this is not necessary and an institution can be made even at a place outside the diocese. But induction should always be after institution, and should not precede it.

The incumbent, once put in possession of his benefice, has within it, subject only to the rights of the bishop and his officers, the exclusive duty of ministering and the exclusive rights to the emoluments appertaining to the cure.

(d) *Conduct of Services*

The incumbent is responsible for the performance of

[1] The modern form of the declaration of assent is set out in Canon C15, (amended as authorised by the Church of England (Worship and Doctrine) Measure 1974). Briefly, it affirms the declarant's belief in and loyalty to the faith revealed in Scripture and set forth in the Creeds, to which the historic formularies of the Church of England (viz. the Articles of Religion, the Book of Common Prayer and the Ordinal) bear witness; and it includes an undertaking to use only the forms of service authorised by canon.

Until recently, a declaration against simony was also required by law, but this requirement has now been abolished.

[2] In certain cases of clergymen who are not citizens of the United Kingdom and Colonies, the bishop has power to dispense with the oath of allegiance.

divine service in his parish. In the absence of reasonable hindrance he is bound to provide that Morning and Evening Prayer daily, and on appointed days the Litany, are said in the church, or one of the churches, of which he is the minister; also (unless dispensed by the bishop) that, in every parish church within his cure, Morning and Evening Prayer are said or sung at least on all Sundays and principal feast days, and on Ash Wednesday and Good Friday. Unless dispensed by the bishop, he must celebrate, or cause to be celebrated, the Holy Communion on all Sundays and greater feast days and on Ash Wednesday; and he must administer the sacraments and other rites (including baptisms, marriages and funerals) as occasion requires. Except for reasonable cause approved by the bishop, he must preach or cause to be preached a sermon at least once each Sunday (see Canons B11, C24).

The incumbent, in addition to the services which he is bound to hold in church, may hold services at other times or in other places. Without the bishop's permission, however, he may not, in strict law, celebrate the Holy Communion, save when visiting the sick of his parish, including those outside the parish who are on his electoral roll.

As to forms of services, the position is now regulated by the Church of England (Worship and Doctrine) Measure 1974, and canons made thereunder.

Under the Measure, the General Synod is authorised to make provision by canon with respect to worship in the Church, including provision for empowering the Synod to approve, amend, continue or discontinue forms of service; and also has power to make provision by canon, or by regulation made thereunder, for any matter, except the publication of banns, to which any of the rubrics of the Prayer Book relate. For the purposes of the Measure, the word 'rubrics' is defined to include all directions and instructions contained in the Prayer Book, and all tables, prefaces, rules, calendars and other contents thereof.

These general powers are, however, subject to the

following limitations and conditions imposed by the Measure:

(1) They must be exercised in such a way as to ensure that the forms of service contained in the Prayer Book will continue to be available for use.

(2) Any canon or regulation made under the powers in question, and any approval, amendment, continuance or discontinuance of a form of service, must be finally approved by the General Synod with a two-thirds majority in each House.

(3) Any canon or regulation so made, and any form of service so approved (whether in its original or an amended form) must be such as in the opinion of the General Synod is neither contrary to, nor indicative of any departure from, the doctrine of the Church of England in any essential matter; but the final approval by the Synod of the canon or regulation or form of service (with the requisite majority in each House) will be conclusive that this requirement is satisfied.

(4) The Measure requires it to be laid down by canon that in the case of approved services other than occasional offices, the decision as to which form of service is to be used in any church in a parish is to be taken jointly by the incumbent and the parochial church council; and further, that if they disagree, the forms to be used shall be those contained in the Prayer Book, unless other approved forms of service have been in regular use in the church during at least two of the four years immediately preceding the disagreement, and the parochial church council resolves that those other forms of service shall be used either to the exclusion of, or in addition to, the forms contained in the Prayer Book.

(5) The Measure also requires it to be laid down by canon that, in the case of occasional offices (other than Con-

firmation), the decision as to which form of service is to be used will be made by the minister who is to conduct the service, but that if any of the persons concerned objects beforehand to the use of the service selected by the minister, and he and the minister cannot agree, the matter is to be referred to the bishop for decision.

These provisions of the Measure have been implemented by Canons B 2, B 3 and B 4A.

Canon B 2 enables the General Synod (by the requisite majority in each House) to approve forms of service either with or without time-limit, and to amend, discontinue, or extend the time-limit on any such form of service, but so that any form of service (as approved or amended) shall be such as in the opinion of the Synod is neither contrary to, nor indicative of any departure from, the doctrine of the Church of England in any essential matter.

Canon B 3 lays down, in accordance with the requirements of the Measure, the manner of deciding which forms of service are to be used in any church in a parish.

Canon B 4A enables the Synod to approve new forms of Collects and Tables of Lessons for use in any service approved under Canon B 2; and also to approve a Table of Rules for regulating the service when two Holy Days fall on the same day or their proper services otherwise fall together, or when necessary for any other reason.

The Alternative Service Book 1980 was authorised by the General Synod under the Measure.

Canons B 4 and B 5, made in exercise of a power expressly conferred by the Measure, contain provision for services on special occasions. Under Canon B 4, the Convocations of Canterbury and York (within their respective provinces), or failing any authorisation by them, the archbishops within their provinces or the bishops within their dioceses may authorise special forms of service for use on occasions for which no provision is made by the Prayer

Book or by the General Synod under Canon B 2; and under Canon B 5, on occasions for which no provision is made either in the Prayer Book, or under Canon B 2, or by Convocation or the archbishops or the diocesan bishop under Canon B 4, the minister may use any form of service he considers suitable. But the exercise of the power conferred on a bishop or a minister by these provisions is subject to any regulations from time to time made by the Convocation of the province.

Canon B 5 also empowers a minister in his discretion to make variations not of substantial importance in any authorised form of service (whether Prayer Book or otherwise) according to particular circumstances.

As regards forms of service contained in the Prayer Book, the Prayer Book (Versions of the Bible) Measure 1965 provides that where any portion of Scripture (that is, a portion from the Authorised Version) is appointed by the Prayer Book to be read said or sung, the corresponding portion of Scripture contained in any version of the Bible for the time being authorised for the purpose by the General Synod may be used at the discretion of the minister, provided (in the case of a church in a parish) that the parochial church council agrees, and also provided (in the case of any occasional office) that none of the persons concerned objects beforehand to its use. The versions at present authorised for this purpose are the Revised and the Revised Standard Versions, the New English Bible, the Jerusalem Bible and the Good News Bible; and also in the case of the Psalms (by express provision of the Measure itself) the Revised Psalter.

The dress of a minister at divine service is laid down by Canon B 8. At Morning and Evening Prayer he is to wear cassock, surplice and scarf; and for occasional offices cassock, surplice and either scarf or stole. At the Holy Communion he is enjoined to wear with the cassock either a surplice with scarf or stole, or a surplice or alb with stole and cope, or an alb with the customary vestments. On any appropriate occasion he may wear a cope; and when he wears a scarf, he may also wear, if a graduate, the hood of his degree. But he is not to change the form of vesture in use in the church in which he officiates without first ascertaining, by consultation with the parochial church council, that such change will be acceptable; in case of disagreement he is to refer the matter to the bishop, whose direction must be obeyed.

(e) *Incumbent's other Duties*

Other duties of the incumbent, as specified in Canon C 24, include the instruction of children; the preparation and presentation to the bishop of confirmation candidates; visiting, particularly of the sick and infirm; and availability to parishioners for spiritual counsel and advice.

The incumbent is under a duty to reside in the parsonage house if there is one, but he may obtain the bishop's licence to live in another fit house, or even outside his parish. He must reside in the parish, unless so licensed, for nine months out of the twelve.

It is the duty of the incumbent to convene the annual parochial church meeting, and if he is present, he acts as chairman. He is also chairman of the parochial church council and, as such, responsible for convening its meetings. He is responsible, jointly with the parochial church council, for the allocation of any money collected in church.[1]

(f) *Enforcement of Duties*

The proceedings which can be taken under the Ecclesiastical Jurisdiction Measure 1963 against an incumbent (or against any other priest or deacon holding a position involving duties) for serious, persistent or continuous neglect of duty are considered in Chapter 2 *ante*.

[1] See p. 73 and p. 150, footnote 1 *post*.

There are also certain special provisions under other statutes for the enforcement of particular duties. In particular, under the Pluralities Act 1838, if, not having the necessary licence from the bishop, an incumbent fails to reside in the parish for the required period in each year, he is liable to forefeit a proportionate part of the annual value of the benefice, and if he continues to be non-resident against the bishop's order, the profits of the benefice may be sequestrated by the bishop. Further, if such a sequestration remains in force during the incumbent's absence without leave for a whole year, the benefice becomes automatically vacant.

The Incumbents (Vacation of Benefices) Measures 1977 deals with cases where there has been a serious breakdown in pastoral relationships within a parish, or where an incumbent is unable, by reason of age or infirmity, to discharge his duties adequately.

In cases of serious breakdown, the effect of the Measure can be summarised as follows:

(i) The procedure for which the Measure provides will be set in motion by a written request to the bishop for an inquiry into the pastoral position in a parish, on the ground that there has been a serious breakdown of the pastoral relationships between the incumbent and his parishioners, to which the conduct of the incumbent or of his parishioners or of both has contributed over a substantial period.

(ii) Such a request may be made either by the incumbent himself, or by the archdeacon, or by a majority of at least two-thirds of the lay members of the parochial church council (in which last-mentioned case the complainants must specify two of their number to act as their representatives, and must indicate which of those two will act as 'the designated representative', i.e. will handle the correspondence relating to the inquiry).

(iii) Unless the request was made by the archdeacon himself, the bishop will direct the archdeacon to use his endeavours to effect a reconciliation, and within six weeks after receiving this direction the archdeacon must report to the bishop whether in his opinion an inquiry should be instituted.

(iv) If either (a) the original request for an inquiry was made by the archdeacon, or (b) the archdeacon reports that in his opinion an inquiry should be instituted, or (c) the archdeacon, though he did not originally so report, informs the bishop within six months after reporting that he considers that the circumstances are such that an enquiry is nevertheless required, the bishop is bound to direct an inquiry unless the incumbent has been in office for less than three years (in which case the bishop has a discretion whether to direct an inquiry or not). If the archdeacon reports against an inquiry, but within six months after his so reporting the secretary of the parochial church council or the 'designated representative' informs the bishop that an inquiry is nevertheless required, the bishop may direct an inquiry but is not obliged to do so.

(v) Any inquiry will be conducted, at the incumbent's option, either by a diocesan committee or by a provincial tribunal. A diocesan committee consists of three clergymen beneficed in or licensed to parishes in the diocese, together with three lay persons on the electoral rolls of parishes in the diocese. A provincial tribunal consists of (a) the chairman, who must be either the chancellor of some other diocese within the same province, or a Queen's Counsel who is a communicant member of the Church of England; (b) two clergymen beneficed in or licensed to parishes in other dioceses within the province; and (c) two lay persons who are communicant members of the Church of England resident in other dioceses within the province. In either case, the inquiry is a judicial process, for which detailed rules of procedure are laid down by the Measure. The findings of the committee or tribunal must be announced in public.

(vi) It is the duty of the committee or tribunal ro report whether in its opinion there has been a serious breakdown of pastoral relationships, and whether the breakdown is one to which the conduct of the incumbent or his parishioners or both has contributed over a substantial period. The report must include recommendations as to the action to be taken by the bishop.

(vii) If, but only if, the committee or tribunal so recommends, the bishop will execute a declaration declaring the benefice vacant as from a date not less than three or more than six months after the date of the declaration. Pending that date, the incumbent is disqualified from exercising any of the functions of his office without the consent of the bishop, and the bishop will make such other provision as he thinks fit for the performance of those functions. The Measure provides, in such a case, for compensation to the incumbent for the loss of his office and for consequential expenses.

(viii) If the committee or tribunal, though without making a recommendation for the vacation of the benefice, attributes blame to the incumbent for the breakdown, the bishop may rebuke the incumbent, and also has power to disqualify him from exercising any of the functions of his office for such period as may be specified (other provision being made as above).

(ix) If the committee or tribunal attributes blame to the parishioners, the bishop may rebuke such of the parishioners as he thinks fit.

(x) Alternatively to reporting in accordance with (vi) above, the committee or tribunal may report that the incumbent is unable by reason of age or infirmity to discharge his duties adequately, with appropriate recommendations, and if it so reports, the same results will follow as if the inquiry had originally been directed to that matter (see below).

(xi) At any time before the bishop notifies the incumbent of the action to be taken as a result of the inquiry, the incumbent may voluntarily resign his benefice with the bishop's consent, and if he does so he will have the same right to compensation as mentioned in (vii) above.

An inquiry on the ground of an incumbent's incapacity, arising from age or infirmity, can only be instituted on the bishop's own instructions. It is conducted by a diocesan committee of inquiry, according to the same rules of procedure as are mentioned above. It is the duty of the committee to report whether, in its opinion, the incumbent is unable by reason of age or infirmity of mind or body to discharge adequately the duties attaching to his benefice, and, if so, to make recommendations as to the action to be taken by the bishop. If, but only if, the committee so recommends, the bishop may notify the incumbent that it is desirable that he should resign his benefice, and if the incumbent then refuses to do so, the bishop must declare the benefice vacant. Other powers vested in the bishop, if the committee makes a positive report, are to appoint an assistant curate with the incumbent's consent, or to give the incumbent leave of absence not exceeding two years (making provision for the discharge of the incumbent's duties during that period); or to make other temporary provision for the discharge of the incumbent's duties. If the incumbent, having been requested to do so, does not consent to the appointment of an assistant curate, the bishop must declare the benefice vacant. If the benefice is vacated under any of the above-mentioned provisions, the incumbent is accorded special pension rights.

(g) *Avoidance of Benefice*

When an incumbent ceases to serve the duties of the cure,

this is said to be an 'avoidance of the benefice'. This may occur by death, resignation, exchange, cession or deprivation, or by compulsory retirement on the ground of age, or by a declaration by the bishop under the Incumbents (Vacation of Benefices) Measure 1977. It also occurs if a sequestration of the profits of the benefice, consequent upon the incumbent's non-residence, continues for a full year, during the continued absence of the incumbent.

In order to effect an exchange the incumbents must obtain the consent of the respective patrons and diocesan bishops. Cession takes place when an incumbent is created a diocesan bishop, or when he is appointed to another benefice or preferment which he cannot lawfully hold with the benefice already held by him at the time of his appointment (in this connection, the Pastoral Measure 1983 provides that, in general, no person can hold benefices in plurality except in pursuance of a pastoral scheme or order, and that no person can hold a cathedral preferment with a benefice unless the cathedral statutes so provide or allow). Deprivation takes effect where there has been simony in connection with the presentation, institution, collation or admission to the benefice, whether the incumbent was or was not a party thereto, or where the incumbent was disqualified from holding the benefice, or by a censure of deprivation pronounced by the bishop or the court (under the Ecclesiastical Jurisdiction Measure 1963) for an offence by the incumbent.

A compulsory retirement age for incumbents and for certain other office-holders (including archbishops, diocesan and suffragan bishops, archdeacons, vicars in team ministries and vicars of guild churches) was imposed for the first time by the Ecclesiastical Offices (Age Limit) Measure 1975. Under this Measure, any office-holder to whom it applies is normally compelled to vacate his office on attaining the age of 70, but in the case of an incumbent the bishop of the diocese may, on grounds of pastoral need, and with the consent of the parochial church council or councils concerned, from time to time authorise his continuance in office for any extended period or periods not exceeding two years in all (so that the retiring age for an incumbent who is granted the maximum extension is 72). The Measure does not apply to any office-holder in respect of an office which he already held on the 1st January 1976 (on which date the Measure came into force).[1]

An incumbent ceases to have any rights to the emoluments of his benefice on the date when his incumbency ceases. When, however, an incumbent dies and there is a parsonage house attached to the benefice, his widow may continue to reside in the house for two calendar months.

(h) *Sequestrations*

When a vacancy occurs in a benefice a process of sequestration is normally issued by the bishop, and some description of this process may therefore not be considered out of place here. Under it, the income of the benefice is ordered to be taken by the sequestrators and applied by them in manner required by the circumstances of the case. There may be a sequestration if the incumbent becomes of unsound mind, or for the recovery of a judgment debt from him or on his bankruptcy, or in certain other cases,[2] as well as when a benefice becomes vacant.

In the case of a vacancy, it was until recently the normal practice to appoint the churchwardens of the parish as sequestrators, but other arrangements are now becoming

[1] Where a person is designated by a pastoral scheme or order as the holder of an office, who was on the 1st January 1976 the incumbent of a benefice affected by the scheme or order, and who continued so to be until the coming into operation of the scheme or order, he is to be deemed (in effect) to have held the designated office continuously from the 1st January 1976 inclusive, and thus to be exempted from compulsory retirement: Church of England (Miscellaneous Provisions) Measure 1978, s. 2.

[2] For other examples, see pp. 13 and 39 *et seq.*

quite usual. It is believed that the present practice in this respect varies to some extent in different dioceses.

Until the coming into force of the Endowments and Glebe Measure 1976, the income receivable by the sequestrators included the income of the endowments of the benefice and of the glebe land (if any) belonging to it. But the effect of the Measure has been, in general, to substitute for these former sources of an incumbent's income a fixed annuity, which ceases to be payable during a vacancy in the benefice. In the result, apart from a few exceptional cases, the income of the benefice coming to the sequestrators during a vacancy will normally consist only of the marriage, burial and other fees which would have been payable to the incumbent if there had been one. In so far as these items are insufficient to meet the sequestrators' expenses, such expenses will be defrayed out of the diocesan stipends fund. Subject as mentioned below in the case of a benefice the right of presentation to which has been suspended, the sequestrators, at the close of the sequestration, will pay any balance in their hands, as certified by the bishop or some person authorised by him, to the Church Commissioners for allocation to the income account of the fund.

If there is in the parish a licensed assistant curate at the time when the vacancy occurs, he continues in office. If there is no assistant curate, or if he is unable by himself to perform all the duties of the cure, the bishop may appoint a priest-in-charge to minister during the vacancy; the sequestrators may themselves employ and pay clergy for the purpose if the bishop does not act.

When the right of presentation to a benefice is in suspense (see p. 58 *post*), the Pastoral Measure, 1983, s. 68 and Schedule 7, makes the following special provisions about sequestration:

(i) A process of sequestration must issue to cover the whole of the period of suspension, and the bishop must ensure that one of the sequestrators whom he appoints is specially qualified by training or experience to discharge the duties efficiently.

(ii) If the period of suspension immediately follows a period when the benefice has been vacant, any sequestrators appointed during the vacancy are to pay over any balance in their hands to the sequestrators appointed for the period of suspension.

(iii) The last-mentioned sequestrators must at the close of the sequestration, or from time to time during the sequestration, account for any balance in their hands to the Church Commissioners; such balance must be allocated by the Commissioners to the income account of the diocesan stipends fund.

(2) THE UNBENEFICED CLERGY

(a) *Generally*

Every person in holy orders who does not hold a benefice is said to be 'unbeneficed'. There are many such persons (e.g. retired clergy and clergy in full-time teaching or administrative posts) who have no parochial responsibilities of their own. A clergyman in this position may (and frequently does) hold the bishop's licence or permission to officiate in the diocese in which he lives, and if so, he may properly be invited to officiate in any church in the diocese where his help is needed.

But the unbeneficed clergy with which this book is chiefly concerned are those who are formally attached to specific parishes or benefices. They fall into two classes: first, ministers in charge of benefices which for the time being lack the services of any incumbent (generally called 'curates-in-charge' or 'priests-in-charge'); and secondly assistant curates, viz. clergymen appointed to assist incumbents within their parishes. It should be noted that neither of these classes of clergy are affected by the Ecclesiastical Officers (Age Limit) Measure 1975; thus there is no age-limit either on their appointment or on their tenure of office.

Before considering these two classes in detail, some explanation may be useful of the expressions 'curate', 'assistant curate', 'curate-in-charge' and 'priest-in-charge', which can give rise to confusion:

(i) 'Curate', in its strict and original sense, means a clergyman who has the 'cure' or care of a parish, i.e. the incumbent or other minister in charge; the word has this meaning in (for example) the rubrics of the Prayer Book. A clergyman whose function if to assist the 'curate' (in the strict sense) is properly not himself a 'curate', but an 'assistant curate'.

(ii) Nevertheless, the practice of referring to an assistant curate simply as a 'curate', though historically and etymologically inaccurate, is now so universal that this has become the normally accepted meaning of the word: so much so that to use the word 'curate' of a clergyman holding any other position may be misleading.

(iii) It is incorrect to refer to an assistant curate, informally attached by his incumbent to a chapel-of-ease, as the 'curate-in-charge'; this is a mere matter of arrangement of duties within the parish, and the legal status of the assistant curate is unaffected. But 'curate-in-charge' is a correct description of an unbeneficed clergyman formally appointed to the charge of a benefice in the incumbent's absence or where there is no incumbent; such a clergyman may alternatively be referred to as a 'priest-in-charge'.

(iv) 'Curate-in-charge' is also the proper description of an assistant curate of a parish who has been given the care of a conventional district within the parish (see p. 26 *ante*). Because of this other meaning of 'curate-in-charge', and also because the word 'curate' as applied to anyone not an assistant curate can give a wrong impression, it may be thought preferable (as has been done in this book) to use the alternative description 'priest-in-charge' for a clergyman, himself unbeneficed, who has been appointed to the charge of a benefice.

(b) *Priests-in-Charge*

Whenever a benefice is under sequestration, the bishop has power to license a clergyman to be the priest-in-charge of the benefice for so long as the sequestration continues. There are various circumstances in which a sequestration may occur (see for example pp. 39 and 44 *ante*), but by far the most usual case is when a benefice becomes vacant. As soon as the vacancy occurs, a sequestration warrant is normally issued; the sequestration then commences, and the power to appoint a priest-in-charge becomes exercisable.

It is not, however, usually considered necessary to license a priest-in-charge for the comparatively short interval which normally elapses between the vacation of a benefice by one incumbent and the admission of the next. Appointments of priests-in-charge have become much more common than formerly in recent years, partly because it sometimes takes time to find a suitable new incumbent owing to a shortage of clergy, but principally because of the increasing exercise by diocesan bishops of their power under section 67 of the Pastoral Measure 1983 to suspend presentations to benefices (see p. 58 *post*); this power is frequently made use of pending the formulation and bringing into operation of a pastoral scheme for reorganising the benefices and parishes within a particular area, and as a result of its exercise a benefice may well remain vacant over a period of years. In such a case, the appointment of a priest-in-charge is appropriate.

Before being licensed to a benefice, a priest-in-charge takes the oath of canonical obedience to the bishop and makes the declaration of assent (see p. 33 *ante*) before the bishop or his commissary. And on the first Sunday on which he officiates, he must make the declaration of assent in the church or one of the churches in which he is licensed to serve, in the presence of the congregation.

In general, a priest-in-charge has the same duties as an incumbent in relation to the parish or parishes which he serves; and many of the Acts and Measures relating to the functions and duties of an incumbent extend to priests-in-charge by express definition. In particular, a priest-in-charge is in the same position as an incumbent as regards the convening and chairing of meetings of parishioners (for the appointment of churchwardens), of parochial church meetings, and of meetings of the parochial church council, and also for various other purposes such as the disposal of money collected in church, and the provisions of the Church of England (Worship and Doctrine) Measure 1974 and the canons thereunder.

Under the Pastoral Measure 1983, section 68 (3), where a priest-in-charge is appointed for any benefice the presentation to which is suspended, the bishop may require him to reside in the parsonage house. But unless this power is applicable and is actually exercised, a priest-in-charge is not under any obligation to reside in any particular house or within the area of the benefice.

A priest-in-charge's appointment, if not previously determined, will continue so long as the benefice continues to exist and remains under sequestration. But the licence of a priest-in-charge may be withdrawn at any time by the bishop (subject to a right of appeal to the archbishop of the province) after the priest-in-charge has been given an opportunity of being heard. If the priest-in-charge himself wishes to resign, he must give three months' written notice to the bishop, unless the bishop waives this requirement.

There is no legal objection to a clergyman being licensed as priest-in-charge to any number of benefices, nor to an incumbent of one benefice being licensed as priest-in-charge of another benefice.

(c) *Assistant Curates*

The most usual reason for appointing one or more assistant curates to a parish is that the work of the parish is too heavy for a single-handed incumbent.

If not newly ordained to a parish, an assistant curate sometimes comes to it for a short time on trial at the invitation of the incumbent with the permission of the bishop. During this period he has no security of tenure and may be dismissed at the pleasure of the incumbent. In order to gain security, an assistant curate must be licensed to his curacy by the bishop who must be satisfied of his personal fitness. In order to be licensed he must be nominated by the incumbent of the parish in which he is to serve, and if he comes from another diocese he must produce to the bishop a testimonial from the bishop of the diocese in which he was last licensed, setting forth his 'honesty, ability, and conformity to the doctrine, discipline, and worship of the church'.

The licence granted to an assistant curate is an instrument under the seal of the bishop, who thereby confers upon him a security of tenure in the curacy. The licence may be withdrawn at any time by the bishop after he has given the assistant curate an opportunity of being heard, and subject to a right of appeal by the assistant curate to the archbishop of the province. After the licence has been issued, the incumbent has a power to determine on six months' notice the appointment of the assistant curate; but this power may only be exercised with the bishop's consent. A parochial church council, as well as an incumbent, may complain to the bishop as to the conduct of an assistant curate, and the churchwardens can make a presentment to the archdeacon or the bishop at the visitation.

The assistant curate may, on the other hand, resign on giving three months' notice to the incumbent and to the bishop, and in practice it is usual, if any complaint is proposed to be made to higher authority, to give an assistant curate an opportunity of tendering his resignation, unless the grounds of complaint are such as to constitute a scandal. The bishop has power to waive the requirement of notice.

Although the licence granted to an assistant curate usually has no time-limit, the bishop now has power to grant such a licence for a specified term of years, at the end of which, if still on foot, it will expire unless renewed. During the specified term, the curate has the same security of tenure, subject to the same conditions, as under an indefinite licence.

On being licensed the assistant curate takes the oath of canonical obedience to the bishop. He also makes a declaration of assent[1] before the bishop or his commissary, unless he has already made it on his ordination on the same day. And on the first Sunday upon which he officiates in the church or one of the churches of the parish to which he is licensed, he must make the declaration of assent in the presence of the congregation. It is desirable that he should do so in the parish church so that the churchwardens may certify the fact.

Copies of all licences to assistant curates are sent to the churchwardens for safe custody in the parish chest.

(3) MEMBERS OF TEAM AND GROUP MINISTRIES

In the context of a team ministry, the words 'rector' and 'vicar' are used in special senses quite different from their traditional meanings.

The incumbent of the benefice or benefices to which a team ministry extends is always styled 'rector'. His office

[1] See p. 33 *ante*.

may be either a perpetual or 'freehold' office (as in the case of an incumbent of an ordinary benefice) or it may be limited by the pastoral scheme establishing the team ministry to a term of years only, with security of tenure during that term.

The other members of the ministry are styled 'vicars', and the office of vicar must be limited to a specified term of years, with security of tenure during that term. Vicars are chosen by the rector and the bishop jointly. They are appointed by licence of the bishop and publicly admitted in a church in the area of the team ministry.

Under the Ecclesiastical Offices (Age Limit) Measure 1975, vicars in team ministries, if appointed on or after the 1st January 1976, are subject to the same rules as incumbents as to age on appointment and as to compulsory retirement at the age of 70 or upwards (see pp. 32 and 43 *ante*).

The rector is the leader of the team, and has a general responsibility for the cure of souls in the area. But there is power for the pastoral scheme or, subject to the scheme, for the bishop's licence appointing any vicar, to assign to such vicar a special cure of souls in respect of part of the area, or a special responsibility for a particular pastoral function, and further to provide that the special cure or responsibility shall be independent of the rector's general responsibility; and the rector's general responsibility is subject to any special cure or responsibility given to a vicar under these powers. There is also power for the scheme or the licence to assign to a vicar a general responsibility to be shared with the rector for the cure of souls in the area as a whole.

Apart from any exercise of the above-mentioned powers, a vicar, by virtue of his office but subject to his licence, has authority to perform in the area of the team ministry all such offices and services as may be performed by an incumbent.

A group ministry is an association of incumbents, whose

benefices are grouped together to form the area of the ministry. Each incumbent has authority to perform, in the area of every benefice within the group, all such offices and services as may be performed by the incumbent of that benefice; and all the incumbents are under a duty to assist each other, so as to make the best possible provision for the cure of souls throughout the area of the group ministry. But each incumbent, when operating in the area of a benefice other than his own, is bound to comply with the directions of the incumbent of that other benefice.

So long as any benefice is included in a group ministry its incumbent cannot resign from the group without also resigning his benefice.

The special provisions contained in the Pastoral Measure 1983 concerning parochial church meetings and councils, and district church councils, and group councils, within the areas of team and group ministries, include provisions conferring either membership of those bodies, or rights of attendance, on all the clergy participating in any such ministry. The text of the provisions in question is set out in Chapter 10.[1]

[1] See p. 152 *post*.

6

The Patron and Patronage

The right to present or appoint a person to a benefice is known as the right of patronage, and if the right is perpetual it is known as an advowson. The person in whom the right is vested is called the patron. The origin of ecclesiastical patronage is ancient and obscure, but it probably grew up gradually as an incident of the system by which, if a lord founded a church on his demesne, he acquired the right of patronage as the ordinary consequence.

The old law concerning patronage has been substantially altered by the Patronage (Benefices) Measure 1986. Of particular importance is the new procedure for the exercise of rights of presentation to a benefice, in which the parochial church council is involved as well as the patron and the bishop. The provisions of the Measure setting out this procedure, which take effect on 1 January 1989, are printed at the end of the chapter.

The right of patronage is a form of property which the owner is freely entitled to deal with in his lifetime or by his will as he thinks fit, subject to certain legal restrictions. The Patronage (Benefices) Measure 1986, reflecting earlier repealed legislation, declares that a right of patronage is incapable of being sold and any attempt to transfer it for valuable consideration is void. New rights of patronage created under the Pastoral Measure 1983 or the enactments which preceded it are likewise, by express provision, unsaleable.

The Patronage (Benefices) Measure 1986 requires a register to be kept in each diocesan registry of the patrons of all the benefices within the diocese. Under the Measure, notice must be given to the bishop and the diocesan registrar of any proposal to transfer a right of patronage. The bishop's consent to the intended transfer is necessary, but before his consent may be given the parochial church council concerned is allowed one month to make representations. Unless an application for registration is made within twelve months of the date of the execution of the instrument of transfer, it has no effect in law. The personal representatives of a deceased patron do not, however, have to register their interest. They may exercise the right of patronage in place of the deceased if a presentation is to be made while the right is vested in them.

Where the patronage of a benefice belongs to an infant beneficially, the legal right to it is vested in trustees who make the presentation on his behalf. If and so long as a patron is a person of unsound mind the right of presentation passes to the Crown.

The patron of a benefice may be a private person, or any other person or corporation recognised by law, for example the Crown, the Lord Chancellor, the diocesan bishop, a university, or a body of trustees. Every diocese has a diocesan board of patronage with a mixed clerical and lay membership, which exists for the purpose of acquiring and exercising rights of patronage.

When a new benefice is created (by union or otherwise) under a pastoral scheme, the scheme can make whatever provision is thought fit as to the patronage thereof (though regard is to be had to the interests of former patrons whose rights have been extinguished by the scheme); if no express provision is made, the diocesan board of patronage will be the patron. When a pastoral scheme creates a team ministry, the scheme itself may designate the first 'rector'; subject to any such designation, and so long as the team ministry continues, the right of patronage will be exercised either by the bishop (if he was originally the sole patron of the benefice), or (in any other case) by the diocesan board of patronage or a specially constituted board as the scheme may provide. In the case of a group ministry, existing rights of patronage in respect of benefices included in the group are not disturbed, but so long as the group ministry continues, a patron may not exercise his right of presentation without the bishop's approval of the person presented.

If no presentation is made within nine months of the vacancy, the right of presentation passes to the archbishop of the province. Neglect of this kind only affects the patron's right of presentation for that turn, and the general right of patronage remains in the patron.

Under Section 67 of the Pastoral Measure 1983, the bishop may, in the case of a vacant benefice or one which is shortly to become vacant, with the consent of the pastoral committee and after consultation with the patron and with the parochial church council concerned, give notice that, for a period of not more than five years, the patron is not to exercise his right of presentation without the consent of the pastoral committee and the bishop. The period of suspension may thereafter be extended an indefinite number of times, by notice served by the bishop, with the same consent and after the same consultation, from time to time before each current period of suspension expires; but the period is not to be extended for more than five years by any one such notice.

During any period of suspension, there is a sequestration of the profits of the benefice (as to which see p. 44 *ante*).

PATRONAGE (BENEFICES) MEASURE 1986 (SO FAR AS RELATING TO THE EXERCISE OF RIGHTS OF PRESENTATION) WITH NOTES

Notification of Vacancies

7. (1) Subject to section 70 of the Pastoral Measure 1983,[1] where a benefice becomes vacant by reason of the death of the incumbent, the bishop shall, as soon as practicable after he becomes aware of the vacancy, give notice of that fact to the designated officer of the diocese.

(2) Subject to section 70 of the Pastoral Measure 1983,[1] where the bishop is aware that a benefice is shortly to become vacant by reason of resignation or cession,[2] the bishop shall give such notice of that fact as he considers reasonable in all the circumstances to the designated officer of the diocese.

(3) Any notice required to be given to the designated officer under subsection (1) or (2) above shall also be given to the registrar of the diocese, unless he is the designated officer.

(4) As soon as practicable after receiving a notice under subsection (1) or (2) above the designated officer shall send notice of the vacancy to the registered patron of the benefice and to the secretary of the parochial church council of the parish belonging to the benefice; and any such notice shall include such information as may be prescribed.

(5) In this Measure 'the designated officer', in relation to a diocese, means such person as the bishop, after consult-

[1] Section 70 provides that this procedure is not to be adopted where the right of presentation has been suspended or restricted in accordance with the Pastoral Measure 1983.

[2] A vacancy by cession occurs when the incumbent becomes a diocesan bishop or obtains another preferment which he cannot hold with the benefice.

ing the bishop's council, may designate or, if no person is designated, the secretary of the pastoral committee of the diocese.

Provisions as to Declarations of Membership

8. (1) Where the registered patron of a benefice is an individual and is not a clerk in Holy Orders, he shall on receiving notice of a vacancy in the benefice under section 7(4) of this Measure—

(*a*) if able to do so, make a written declaration (in this Measure referred to as 'the declaration of membership') declaring that he is an actual communicant member of the Church of England or of a Church in communion with that Church; or

(*b*) if unable to make the declaration himself, appoint some other person, being an individual who is able and willing to make it or is a clerk in Holy Orders or one of the bodies mentioned in subsection (7) below, to act as his representative to discharge in his place the functions of a registered patron.[1]

(2) Where the registered patron of a benefice is a body of persons corporate or unincorporate then, on receiving notice of a vacancy in the benefice under section 7(4) of this Measure, that body shall appoint an individual who is able and willing to make the declaration of membership or is a clerk in Holy Orders to act as its representative to discharge in its place the functions of a registered patron.

(3) Notwithstanding anything in subsection (1) above, where the registered patron of a benefice who is an individual and is not the bishop of a diocese is of the opinion, on receiving notice of a vacancy in the benefice under section

[1] This provision replaces the old disqualification affecting Roman Catholics; it applies generally to patrons who are not members of the Church of England.

7(4) of this Measure, that he will be unable for any reason to discharge his functions as a patron of that benefice he may, notwithstanding that he is able to make the declaration of membership, appoint such a representative as is mentioned in subsection (1)(*b*) above to discharge those functions in his place.

(4) Where a benefice the right of presentation to which belongs to an office (other than an ecclesiastical office) becomes vacant, the person who holds that office on the date on which the benefice becomes vacant shall be entitled to present on that vacancy and shall as soon as practicable after that date—

(*a*) if able to do so, make the declaration of membership, or

(*b*) if unable to make the declaration himself, appoint some other person, being a person who may be appointed as a representative under subsection (1)(*b*) above, to act as his representative to discharge in his place the functions of a registered patron.

(5) Where the right of presentation to a benefice is exercisable by the donee of a power of attorney,[1] the donee shall as soon as practicable after receiving notice of the vacancy in the benefice (or, if the power is created during the vacancy, as soon as practicable after it is created)—

(*a*) if able to do so, make the declaration of membership, or

(*b*) if unable to make the declaration himself, appoint some other person, being a person who may be appointed as a representative under subsection (1)(*b*) above, to act as his representative to discharge in his place the functions of a registered patron.

[1] A power of attorney is a written instrument whereby a person authorises another (the donee) to act on his behalf.

(6) Where under the preceding provisions of this section a body mentioned in subsection (7) below is appointed to discharge the functions of a registered patron, that body shall as soon as practicable after being so appointed appoint as its representative an individual who is able and willing to make the declaration of membership or is a clerk in Holy Orders.

(7) The bodies referred to in subsection (1)(*b*) above are—

(*a*) the dean and chapter or the cathedral chapter of the cathedral church of the diocese;
(*b*) the dean and chapter of the collegiate church of St Peter in Westminster;
(*c*) the dean and canons of the collegiate church of St George, Windsor;
(*d*) any diocesan board of patronage;
(*e*) any patronage board constituted by a pastoral scheme;
(*f*) any university in England or any college or hall in such a university; and
(*g*) the colleges of Eton and Winchester.

Information to be sent to Designated Officer

9. (1) Before the expiration of the period of two months beginning with the date on which a benefice becomes vacant, a registered patron who is an individual shall send to the designated officer of the diocese—

(*a*) the declaration of membership made by him, or
(*b*) the name and address of his representative and the declaration of membership made by that representative.

(2) Before the expiration of the said period of two months, a registered patron which is a body of persons corporate or unincorporate shall send to the designated officer of the diocese the name and address of the indi-

vidual who is to act as its representative and the declaration of membership made by that representative.

(3) Where the functions of a registered patron are to be discharged by the holder of an office, subsection (1) above shall apply to the person who holds that office on the date on which the benefice becomes vacant as it applies to the registered patron.

(4) Where the functions of a registered patron are to be discharged by the donee of a power of attorney, subsection (1) above shall apply to the donee as it applies to the registered patron except that, if the power is created during the vacancy concerned, there shall be substituted for the period of two months mentioned in that subsection the period of two months beginning with the date on which the power is created, and the information required to be sent under that subsection shall include information as to that date.

(5) Where the registered patron or his representative is a clerk in Holy Orders, the registered patron shall, before the expiration of the period during which the declaration of membership is required to be sent to the designated officer under the preceding provisions of this section, notify the designated officer of that fact, and a declaration of membership made by that clerk shall not be required to be sent to the designated officer under this section.

(6) As soon as practicable after receiving information under this section as to the appointment of a representative, the designated officer shall send to the secretary of the parochial church council the name and address of that representative.

Disqualification for Presentation

10. Where the registered patron of a benefice or the representative of that patron, is a clerk in Holy Orders or is the wife of such a clerk, that clerk shall be disqualified for presentation to that benefice.[1]

Requirements as to Meetings of Parochial Church Council

11. (1) Before the expiration of the period of four weeks beginning with the date on which the notice under section 7(4) of this Measure is sent to the secretary of the parochial church council, one or more meetings of that council shall be held for the purposes of—

(*a*) preparing a statement describing the conditions, needs and traditions of the parish[2]
(*b*) appointing two lay members of the council to act as representatives of the council in connection with the selection of an incumbent;
(*c*) deciding whether to request the registered patron to consider advertising the vacancy;
(*d*) deciding whether to request a meeting under section 12 of this Measure; and
(*e*) deciding whether to request a statement in writing from the bishop describing in relation to the benefice the needs of the diocese and the wider interests of the Church.

(2) A meeting of the parochial church council for which subsection (1) above provides shall be convened by the secretary thereof, and no member of that council who is—

(*a*) the outgoing incumbent or the wife of the outgoing incumbent, or
(*b*) the registered patron, or
(*c*) the representative of the registered patron,

shall attend that meeting.

[1] The purpose of this provision is to prevent a clergyman from acquiring a benefice by obtaining direct control of the right of presentation to it.
[2] There is no longer any prohibition against naming a particular clerk as a candidate for the vacancy.

(3) None of the following members of the parochial church council, that is to say—

(*a*) any person mentioned in subsection (2) above, and
(*b*) any deaconess or lay worker licensed to the parish,

shall be qualified for appointment under subsection (1)(*b*) above.

(4) If before the vacancy in the benefice is filled any person appointed under subsection (1)(*b*) above dies or becomes unable for any reason to act as the representative of, or ceases to be a member of, the council by which he was appointed, then, except where he ceases to be such a member and the council decides that he shall continue to act as its representative, his appointment shall be deemed to have been revoked and the council shall appoint another lay member of the council (not being a member disqualified under subsection (3) above) to act in his place for the remainder of the proceedings under this Part of this Measure.

(5) If a parochial church council holds a meeting under subsection (1) above but does not appoint any representatives at that meeting, then, subject to subsection (6) below, two churchwardens who are members of that council (or, if there are more than two churchwardens who are members of the council, two churchwardens chosen by all the churchwardens who are members) shall act as representatives of the council in connection with the selection of an incumbent.

(6) A churchwarden who is the registered patron of a benefice shall not be qualified under subsection (5) above to act as a representative of the parochial church council or to choose any other churchwarden so to act, and in any case where there is only one churchwarden qualified to act as such a representative that churchwarden may act as the sole representative of that council in connection with the selection of the incumbent.

(7) Any representative of the parochial church council appointed under subsection (1) to (4) above and any churchwarden acting as such a representative by virtue of subsection (5) or (6) above is in this Part of this Measure referred to as a 'parish representative', and where a churchwarden is entitled to act as the sole parish representative any reference in this Part to the parish representatives shall be construed as a reference to that churchwarden.

(8) A copy of the statement prepared under subsection 1(*a*) above together with the names and addresses of the parish representatives shall, as soon as practicable after the holding of the meeting under that subsection, be sent by the secretary of the parochial church council, to the registered patron and, unless the bishop is the registered patron, to the bishop.

Joint Meeting of Parochial Church Council with Bishop and Patron

12. (1) Where a request for a meeting under this section is made—

(*a*) by a notice sent by the registered patron or the bishop to the secretary of the parochial church council, or
(*b*) by a resolution of the parochial church council, passed at a meeting held under section 11 of this Measure,

a joint meeting of the parochial church council with the registered patron and (if the bishop is not the registered patron) the bishop shall be held for the purpose of enabling those present at the meeting to exchange views on the statement prepared under section 11(1)(*a*) of this Measure (needs of the parish) and the statement presented under subsection (2) below (needs of the diocese).

(2) At any meeting held under this section the bishop shall present either orally or, if a request for a statement in writing has been made by the registered patron or the

parochial church council, in writing a statement describing in relation to the benefice the needs of the diocese and the wider interests of the Church.

(3) Any notice given under subsection (1)(*a*) above shall be of no effect unless it is sent to the secretary of the parochial church council not later than ten days after a copy of the statement prepared under subsection (1)(*a*) of section 11 of this Measure is received by the persons mentioned in subsection (8) of that section.

(4) The outgoing incumbent and the wife of the outgoing incumbent shall not be entitled to attend a meeting held under this section.

(5) A meeting requested under this section shall be held before the expiration of the period of six weeks beginning with the date on which the request for the meeting was first made (whether by the sending of a notice as mentioned in subsection (1)(*a*) above or by the passing of a resolution as mentioned in subsection (1)(*b*) above), and at least fourteen days' notice (unless a shorter period is agreed by all the persons concerned) of the time and place at which the meeting is to be held shall be given by the secretary of the parochial church council to the registered patron, the bishop (if he is not the registered patron) and the members of the parochial church council.

(6) If either the registered patron or the bishop is unable to attend a meeting held under this section, he shall appoint some other person to attend on his behalf.

(7) The chairman of any meeting held under this section shall be such person as the persons who are entitled to attend and are present at the meeting may determine.

(8) No meeting requested under this section shall be treated for the purposes of this Measure as having been held unless there were present at the meeting—

(*a*) the bishop or the person appointed by the bishop to attend on his behalf, and
(*b*) the registered patron or the person appointed by the patron to attend on his behalf, and
(*c*) at least one third of the members of the parochial church council who were entitled to attend.

(9) The secretary of the parochial church council shall invite both the rural dean of the deanery in which the parish is (unless he is the outgoing incumbent) and the lay chairman of the deanery synod of that deanery to attend a meeting held under this section.

Provisions with respect to Selection of Incumbent

13. (1) The registered patron of a vacant benefice shall not make to any priest an offer to present him to a benefice until—

(*a*) if a request for a meeting under section 12 of this Measure has been made, either—

(i) that meeting has been held, or
(ii) all the parties concerned have agreed that no such meeting should be held, or
(iii) the period of six weeks mentioned in section 12(5) has expired; and

(*b*) (whether or not such a request has been made) the making of the offer to the priest in question has been approved—

(i) by the parish representatives, and
(ii) if the registered patron is a person other than the bishop of the diocese in which the benefice is, by that bishop.[1]

[1] The effect of this provision is that the bishop (if he is not the patron) or a parish representative may override the patron's choice; but the patron has in those circumstances the right to appeal to the archbishop under subsection (5).

(2) If, before the expiration of the period of four weeks beginning with the date on which the registered patron sent to the bishop a request for him to approve under paragraph (*b*) of subsection (1) above the making of the offer to the priest named in the request, no notice is received from the bishop of his refusal to approve the making of the offer, the bishop shall be deemed to have given his approval under that paragraph.

(3) If, before the expiration of the period of two weeks beginning with the date on which the registered patron sent to the parish representatives a request for them to approve under paragraph (*b*) of subsection (1) above the making of the offer to the priest named in the request, no notice is received from any representative of his refusal to approve the making of the offer, the representatives shall be deemed to have given their approval under that paragraph.

(4) If—

(*a*) the bishop refuses to approve under paragraph (*b*) of subsection (1) above the making of the offer to the priest named in the request, or
(*b*) any parish representative refuses to approve under that paragraph the making of that offer,

the bishop or the representative, as the case may be, shall notify the registered patron in writing of the grounds on which the refusal is made.

(5) Where approval of an offer is refused under subsection (4) above, the registered patron may request the archbishop to review the matter and if, after review, the archbishop authorises the registered patron to make the offer in question, the patron may make that offer accordingly.

(6) Where a priest accepts an offer made in accordance with the provisions of this section to present him to a benefice and the registered patron is a person other than the

bishop, the patron shall send the bishop a notice presenting the priest to him for admission to the benefice.

Failure of Registered Patron to comply with s. 9

14. Where any declaration of membership or other information required to be sent to the designated officer under section 9 of this Measure is not sent to that officer before the expiration of the period during which it is required to be so sent and the registered patron is a person other than the bishop then, after the expiration of that period—

(*a*) no meeting shall be held under section 12 of this Measure by reason of any request made by the registered patron and subsections (2), (5), (6) and (8) of that section shall not apply in relation to that patron; and

(*b*) no offer shall be made to any priest under section 13 of this Measure;

but the bishop may, subject to subsection (2) below, make to such priest as he thinks fit an offer to collate him to the benefice.

(2) The bishop shall not make an offer under subsection (1) above unless the making of the offer has been approved by the parish representatives, and subsections (3), (4)(*b*) and (5) of section 13 of this Measure shall apply in relation to a request sent by the bishop to those representatives by virtue of this subsection as if for any reference to the registered patron there were substituted a reference to the bishop.

(3) Where under subsection (1) above the bishop makes to a priest an offer to collate him to a benefice in respect of which there is more than one person registered under this Measure, the registered patron whose turn it was to present to the benefice shall be treated for the purposes of this Measure as having exercised that turn.

Failure of Council to comply with s. 11 or 12

15. If a copy of the statement prepared under section 11(1)(*a*) of this Measure is not sent under subsection (8) of that section to the persons mentioned in that subsection or if notice is not given under section 12(5) of this Measure of any joint meeting requested under subsection (1)(*a*) of the said section 12 then—

(*a*) if the bishop is the registered patron, he may, without making any request for the approval of the parish representatives, make to such priest as he thinks fit an offer to collate him to the benefice; and

(*b*) if the bishop is not the registered patron, that patron shall be entitled to proceed under section 13 of this Measure as if paragraphs (*a*) and (*b*)(i) of subsection (1), subsection (3) and paragraph (*b*) of subsection (4) thereof had not been enacted.

7

The Office of Churchwarden

The office of churchwarden is a venerable one, which had already emerged into legal recognition by the thirteenth century. Two centuries later the churchwardens were chosen annually in parish meeting, all adult parishioners having a voice in the election. Once elected, the churchwardens normally transacted all parish business during their year of office. They had, in fact, a two-fold significance; they were both guardians of the parochial morals and trustees of the Church's goods.

The functions of churchwardens at the present time are dealt with in the next chapter of this book. This present chapter is concerned with their qualification and manner of appointment, and with the modes whereby the office of churchwarden may be vacated. The law on these subjects is now contained almost entirely in the Churchwardens (Appointment and Resignation) Measure 1964, as amended in some respects by the Synodical Government Measure 1969. The Measure of 1964 is, to a large extent, a restatement in statutory form of the pre-existing law, but it has introduced some changes, the more important of which are mentioned in the notes to the Measure below.

CHURCHWARDENS (APPOINTMENT AND RESIGNATION) MEASURE 1964 (AS AMENDED), WITH NOTES

A Measure passed by the National Assembly of the Church of England to regulate the number and qualifications of, and the time and manner of choosing, churchwardens of parishes; to regulate their admission to office; to provide for the resignation of churchwardens and for their vacating their offices in certain events; to regulate the qualifications of churchwardens of Guild Churches in the City of London; and for purposes connected therewith. [27th February 1964].

Number and qualifications of churchwardens

1. (1) Subject to the provisions of this Measure there shall be two churchwardens of every parish.[1]

(2) The churchwardens of every parish shall be chosen from persons who are resident in the parish or whose names are on the church electoral roll of the parish.

(3) Such persons shall be actual communicant members of the Church of England except where the bishop shall otherwise permit and of twenty-one years of age and upwards.[2]

(4) No person shall be chosen as a churchwarden unless he has signified his consent to serve.[3]

[1] Exceptionally, there may be a different number by custom; see section 12 (2) below. There is now another exception under the Pastoral Measure 1983 where a pastoral scheme designates two or more parish churches in a single parish: see p. 112 footnote *post*.

[2] Previously to the Measure, membership of the Church of England was an essential qualification in new but not in ancient parishes. The requirement of being an 'actual communicant' is entirely new. The qualifying age is still twenty-one, notwithstanding that eighteen is now 'full age' under the general law.

[3] Previously, in ancient parishes, every householder could be made to serve, except for certain classes of persons who were exempted or disqualified.

Time and manner of choosing churchwardens

2. (1) The churchwardens of a parish shall be chosen annually not later than the 30th April in each year.[1]

(2) Subject to the provisions of this Measure the churchwardens of a parish shall be chosen by the joint consent of the minister of the parish and a meeting of the parishioners if it may be; such joint consent shall be deemed to have been signified:—

(*a*) if any motion stating the names of the persons to be chosen as churchwardens or the name of either of them shall be declared by the person presiding over the meeting to have been carried; and

(*b*) if in respect of any such motion the minister shall have announced his consent to the choice of the person or persons named therein either before the putting of the motion to the meeting or immediately upon the declaration of the result thereof:

Provided that no person shall be deemed to have been chosen as a churchwarden under the provisions of this subsection unless both churchwardens have been so chosen.[2]

(3) If the minister of the parish and the meeting of the parishioners cannot agree on the choice of both churchwardens by joint consent as provided in the foregoing subsection or if after due opportunity has been given no motions or insufficient motions have been moved in accordance with the provisions of that subsection then one churchwarden shall be appointed by the minister and the

[1] Printed as amended by the Synodical Government Measure 1969. The original requirement as to time was 'not later in the year than during the week following Easter week'. In practice, the meeting is usually held on the same day as and immediately before the annual parochial church meeting (see p. 96 *post*).

[2] This sub-section reproduces in substance the rule previously obtaining. It is now, as it has always been, incorrect, as is so often the practice, for the incumbent to choose one churchwarden and the parishioners the other, without first attempting to agree to the choice of both.

other shall then be elected by the meeting of the parishioners.

(4) During any period when there is no minister both the churchwardens shall be elected by the meeting of the parishioners.

(5) A person may be chosen to fill a casual vacancy among the churchwardens at any time.

(6) Any person chosen to fill a casual vacancy shall be chosen in the same manner as was the churchwarden in whose place he is appointed.[1]

Meeting of the parishioners

3. (1) A joint meeting of:—

(*a*) the persons whose names are entered on the church electoral roll of the parish; and

(*b*) the persons resident in the parish whose names are entered on a register of local government electors by reason of such residence:

shall be deemed to be a meeting of the parishioners for the purposes of this Measure.

(2) The meeting of the parishioners shall be convened by the minister or the churchwardens of the parish by a notice signed by the minister or a churchwarden.

(3) The notice shall state the place, day and hour at which the meeting of the parishioners is to be held.

(4) The notice shall be affixed on or near to the principal door of the parish church and of every other building

[1] It is conceived that if the churchwarden whose place has to be filled was himself chosen by agreement between minister and parishioners, but they cannot agree on any person to fill the casual vacancy, the vacancy must remain unfilled until the next annual meeting.

licensed for public worship in the parish for a period including the last two Sundays before the meeting.

(5) The minister, if present, or, if he is not present, a chairman chosen by the meeting of the parishioners, shall preside thereat.

(6) In case of an equal division of votes the chairman of the meeting of the parishioners shall have a casting vote.[1]

(7) The meeting of the parishioners shall have power to adjourn, and to determine its own rules of procedure.

(8) A person appointed by the meeting of the parishioners shall act as clerk of the meeting and shall record the minutes thereof.

4, 5 and 6. . . .[2]

Admission of churchwardens

7. (1) At a time and place to be appointed by the ordinary each person chosen for the office of churchwarden shall appear before the ordinary, or his substitute duly appointed, and be admitted to the office of churchwarden after subscribing the declaration that he will faithfully and diligently perform the duties of his office, and making the same in the presence of the ordinary or his substitute. No person chosen for the office of churchwarden shall become

[1] The Synodical Government Measure 1969 provides that this subsection shall not apply to elections of churchwardens. It accordingly now only applies to votes on procedural matters (e.g. a proposal to adjourn).

[2] Sections 4, 5 and 6, relating to the procedure applicable to elections, were repealed by the Synodical Government Measure 1969. These matters are now dealt with by rules 10 and 11 of the Church Representation Rules (see p. 103 *post*).

churchwarden until such time as he shall have been admitted to office in accordance with the provisions of this section.[1]

(2) Subject to the provisions of this Measure the churchwardens so chosen and admitted as aforesaid shall continue in their office until they, or others as their successors, be admitted in like manner before the ordinary.

Resignation of churchwardens

8. (1) If a churchwarden wishes to resign his office he may, with the consent in writing of the minister and any other churchwarden of the parish, resign his office by an instrument in writing addressed to the bishop, and if the bishop accepts his resignation his office shall forthwith be vacated.

(2) Subject to the provisions of this section a churchwarden shall not be entitled to resign his office.[2]

[1] The admission of churchwardens, after subscribing the declaration referred to in this sub-section, ordinarily takes place at the annual 'visitation'. It is usual for a bishop to 'visit' his diocese from time to time, and in those years when he does not do so a visitation is held, on his behalf, by the archdeacon in each archdeaconry. In the case of an episcopal visitation the admission takes place before the bishop or his chancellor or surrogate. In other years it is performed by the archdeacon or his official. It is open to any person to allege that some cause exists why the persons claiming admission should not be admitted to office; and the bishop or archdeacon, as the case may be, may make inquiries before admitting a person even if no such cause is alleged. But any refusal to admit a person as churchwarden must be on the ground of some definite legal disqualification (e.g. that he is under due age, or that he is neither resident in the parish nor on its electoral roll), and not on any such ground as (e.g.) alleged unfitness for moral or other reasons. The remedy for a refusal to admit is by proceedings in the High Court of Justice.

It should be stressed that a newly appointed churchwarden is not in office until actually admitted. If he is prevented by illness or other good reason from attending the visitation, he may be admitted by arrangement before a surrogate.

[2] Previously to the Measure, the question whether a churchwarden could validly resign was doubtful.

Vacation of office

9. The office of churchwarden shall be vacated if the churchwarden is not resident in the parish and if his name is not on the church electoral roll of the parish.[1]

Guild Churches

10. (1) In the case of every church in the City of London designated and established as a Guild Church under the City of London (Guild Churches) Acts, 1952 and 1960, the churchwardens shall, notwithstanding anything to the contrary contained in those Acts, be actual communicant members of the Church of England except where the bishop shall otherwise permit.

(2) Subject to the provisions of subsection (1) of this section, nothing in this Measure shall apply to the churchwardens of any church designated and established as a Guild Church under the City of London (Guild Churches) Acts 1952 and 1960.[2]

Special provisions

11. (1) In the carrying out of this Measure in any diocese the bishop of such diocese shall have power:—

(*a*) to make provision for any matter not herein provided for;

(*b*) to appoint a person to do any act in respect of which there has been any neglect or default on the part of any

[1] This is a new provision.

[2] As to guild churches generally, see p. 28 *ante*. Under the Act of 1952, the churchwardens of a guild church (two in number) are chosen by the vicar and members of the guild church electoral roll at an annual guild church meeting held in each year before Low Sunday. Eligible candidates are persons who are either on the guild church electoral roll, or eligible to be churchwardens of some parish in the City of London.

person or body charged with any duty under this Measure;

(*c*) so far as may be necessary for the purpose of giving effect to the intentions of this Measure, to extend or alter the time for holding any meeting or election or to modify the procedure laid down by this Measure in connection therewith;

(*d*) in any case in which there has been no valid choice to direct a fresh choice to be made, and to give such directions in connection therewith as he may think necessary; and

(*e*) in any case in which any difficulty arises, to give any directions which he may consider expedient for the purpose of removing the difficulty.

(2) The powers of the bishop under this section shall not enable him to validate anything that was invalid at the time it was done.

(3) . . .[1]

(4) During a vacancy in a diocesan see the powers by this section conferred upon a bishop of the diocese shall be exercisable by the guardian of the spiritualities.[2]

Savings

12. (1) Subject to the provisions of section ten of this Measure, nothing in this Measure shall be deemed to amend, repeal or affect any local act or any scheme made under any enactment affecting the churchwarden of a parish:

Provided that for the purposes of this Measure the Parish of Manchester Division Act, 1850, shall be deemed to be a general act.

[1] This sub-section, which related to the form of voting paper to be used at elections, was repealed by the Synodical Government Measure 1969. See now the Church Representation Rules, rules 10 and 11 (p. 103 *post*).

[2] See pp. 1, 2 *ante*.

(2) In the case of any parish where there is an existing custom which regulates the number of churchwardens or the manner in which the churchwardens are chosen, nothing in this Measure shall affect that custom;[1]

Provided that in the case of any parish, where in accordance with that custom any churchwarden is chosen by the vestry of that parish either alone or jointly with any other person or persons that churchwarden shall be chosen by the meeting of the parishioners, either alone or jointly with the other person or persons, as the case may be.

(3) Nothing in this Measure shall affect a churchwarden in office before the passing of this Measure during the period for which he was chosen.

(4) Nothing in this Measure shall be deemed to authorise the choice of any person as churchwarden who under the existing law is disqualified from being chosen for that office.[2]

Interpretation

13. In this Measure, except in so far as the context otherwise requires:—

'existing custom' means a custom existing at the commencement of this Measure which has continued for a period including the last forty years before its commencement.[3]

'Rules for the Representation of the Laity' means the

[1] Instances of local customs are numerous. There can be a valid custom whereby there may be only one churchwarden, or three or more churchwardens, for a parish, or whereby churchwardens are elected for separate parts of the parish. In most ancient parishes in the City of London, there is a custom whereby both churchwardens are chosen by the parishioners.

[2] Aliens, also persons who have been convicted of certain criminal offences, are amongst those who are disqualified.

[3] i.e. the last forty years before 1st January 1965; see section 15 (3). The forty years' qualification period was presumably imposed in order to prevent the continuation or revival of doubtful or half-forgotten customs.

Rules for the Representation of the Laity[1] contained in the Schedule to the Representation of the Laity Measure, 1956;

'actual communicant member,' 'minister,' 'parish' and 'public worship' have the same meanings respectively as those assigned to those expressions in Rule 1 of the Rules for the Representation of the Laity.[1]

14. . . .[2]

Short title, extent and commencement

15. (1) This Measure may be cited as the Churchwardens (Appointment and Resignation) Measure, 1964.

(2) This Measure shall extend to the whole of the provinces of Canterbury and York except for the Channel Islands and the Isle of Man:

Provided that—

(*a*) this Measure may be applied to the Channel Islands as defined in the Channel Islands (Church Legislation) Measures, 1931 and 1957, or either of them in accordance with those Measures:

(*b*) if an Act of Tynwald so provides this Measure shall extend to the Isle of Man subject to such modifications, if any, as may be specified in such Act of Tynwald.

(3) This Measure shall come into force on the first day of January next after the date on which it receives the Royal Assent.[3]

[1] The Rules for the Representation of the Laity have been replaced by the Church Representation Rules. The relevant definitions are now contained in Rule 44 of the last-mentioned Rules (p. 126 *post*).

[2] Section 14 merely repealed certain previous enactments and it is unnecessary to reproduce it here.

[3] i.e. 1st January 1965.

8

The Functions of Churchwardens

(1) Churchwardens and Chapelwardens—(2) Powers and Duties: (*a*) As to Church, Churchyard and Contents of Church; (*b*) Maintenance of Order; (*c*) Allocation of Seats; (*d*) Alms and Collections; (*e*) Vacancy of Benefice; (*f*) Churchwardens as Bishops' Officers—(3) Actions by and against Churchwardens.

(1) CHURCHWARDENS AND CHAPELWARDENS

In this chapter it is proposed to consider the functions of churchwardens after their admission to office. These functions extend to every consecrated church and chapel within the parish. While it is usual to have wardens in a chapel-of-ease, these (unless appointed in accordance with one or other of the statutory provisions mentioned below) do not as such have any legal status, nor can they act as *church*wardens unless the churchwardens of the parish give them the authority to do so; and even in that case they act only as the agents of the churchwardens. It is desirable, therefore, that such wardens should be appointed as sidesmen of the parish church, by which means they may be given a legal status as officers of the parish, with the duty of assisting the churchwardens in the exercise of their office.

Under rule 16 of the Church Representation Rules,[1] a procedure is laid down which, if it is followed, enables a 'district church council' to be constituted, and 'deputy churchwardens' to be elected or chosen, for any church or place of worship situated within a parish. And under the Pastoral Measure 1983,[2] in the case of a team ministry established by a pastoral scheme, provision can be made for the election (similar to that contemplated by rule 16 of the Church Representation Rules) of a 'district church council' and 'deputy churchwardens' for any district in the parish which contains a church or place of worship. There is power to delegate particular functions to the deputy churchwardens under both rule 16 and the Measure.

Reference may also here be made to the case of a parish which by virtue of a pastoral scheme has two or more parish churches, each with its set of two churchwardens. Such churchwardens may, if they think fit, arrange to perform separate duties in relation to the several parish churches.[3]

It may be mentioned in passing that if the 'wardens' of a chapel-of-ease undertake the care of the funds of the congregation, or of moneys raised by the congregation for a particular purpose such as the maintenance of the fabric, they thereby constitute themselves trustees of the funds or moneys in question, and will be answerable for their proper expenditure. But they are not personally liable on a contract unless they bind themselves expressly.

(2) POWERS AND DUTIES

(a) *As to Church, Churchyard and Contents of Church*

The incumbent is the person in whom the freehold of church and churchyard is normally vested. But possession of both is vested in the incumbent and churchwardens jointly, and if

[1] See p. 110 *post* for the text of this provision.
[2] See p. 153 *post* for the text of this provision.
[3] See p. 112 footnote *post*.

any person claims to enter a church for any purpose other than assisting at a service, the incumbent and church-wardens together have the right to prevent him.

While the incumbent has the custody of the key of the church, the churchwardens have the right of access to the church for the proper discharge of their duties.

All the movable furniture and ornaments of the church are in the legal ownership of the churchwardens, but the clergy must be allowed any use of these objects which is necessary for their ministrations. The churchwardens must not remove furnishings or ornaments or introduce new ones without a faculty or an archdeacon's certificate[1] unless such action amounts merely to replacing any article which is worn out, and even this should only be done in consultation with the incumbent. If any article is stolen, the churchwardens may take all the steps necessary for its recovery and for the prosecution of the thief.

The care, maintenance, preservation and insurance of the fabric of the church, and of the goods and ornaments thereof, and the repair of the churchyard fence and other structures, are, under the modern law, the responsibility of the parochial church council and not of the churchwardens as such.

(b) *Maintenance of Order*

It is the duty of churchwardens to maintain order in the church and churchyard, especially during divine service. They may remove persons who disturb the performance of the service, or who show that they intend to do so. Thus, it has been held that a churchwarden could properly remove a man's hat if he refused to remove it during divine service after being requested to do so.

It is a criminal offence at common law to strike any person in a church or churchyard. And, under the Ecclesiastical

1 See Chapter 3 *ante*.

Courts Jurisdiction Act 1860, riotous, violent, or indecent behaviour in any church, churchyard or burial ground is an offence punishable by fine or imprisonment; so also is the disturbance of a duly authorised preacher, or of any clergyman celebrating any sacrament or divine service. Any person offending under this Act may be arrested by any constable or churchwarden of the parish or place.

These provisions apply to clergy and laity alike. It is to be observed, however, that the churchwardens cannot interfere with the conduct of the services by the minister unless his behaviour is such as to bring him within the purview of the Act. In any other case they have no remedy except by way of complaint to the bishop.

(c) *Allocation of Seats*

Churchwardens are entrusted with the duty of providing seats for the parishioners. In this capacity they act as the officers of the bishop, who at common law had the right of disposal of the seats. Their rights and duties in this respect may be limited by some over-riding right of a private person, e.g. when a particular pew is attached to an estate by prescription.[1] Subject, however, to any such rights as these, and subject also, in a church where there are pew-rents, to the rights of the pew-holders, the churchwardens may direct persons where to sit, and where not to sit, and may do this beforehand or for a particular service or for an indefinite period. But they cannot legally give the right to a particular seat for all time, because to do so would divest themselves or their successors of the liberty to rearrange the seating accommodation at a future time. Seats can legally be assigned only to parishioners, and before dispossessing a parishioner of a seat normally occupied by him, the churchwardens would be well advised to give him notice of their

[1] Or faculty.

intention, in order that he may show cause why he should not be so dispossessed.

This control of the seating accommodation belongs to the churchwardens in the interests of good order. They cannot exclude an orderly person on the ground that the church is full if he can stand in such a part of the church as will not interfere with the conduct of the service. It is illegal to demand payment, by way of rent or otherwise, for the exclusive use of a seat, unless there is express statutory permission applicable to the church in question. If a parishioner intrudes himself into a seat contrary to the directions of the churchwardens, they may remove him, provided that they do not use unnecessary force or cause a scandal by disturbing the worship of the church.

(d) *Alms and Collections*

Formerly the minister and churchwardens were entrusted with the disposal, for pious and charitable uses, of alms given at the Communion Service. The rubric in the Book of Common Prayer conferring this authority upon them has, however, been overruled by Canon B17A. As a result Communion alms are now to be treated in the same way as other collections. The power of allocating all collections now rests, under section 7 of the Parochial Church Councils (Powers) Measure 1956, with the incumbent and the parochial church council; the churchwardens as such are not concerned.

Presumably the churchwardens' duties with respect to collections are confined to receiving the money, and holding it (until handed over to the treasurer or other authorised person) as agents for the incumbent and the council.

(e) *Vacancy of Benefice*

Immediately a benefice becomes vacant from any cause other than the resignation of the incumbent, the churchwardens should notify the bishop and the patron. Upon the occurrence of any vacancy, the bishop will probably cause a sequestration warrant to be issued, whereby sequestrators will be appointed (who may or may not be the churchwardens of the parish). The effect of sequestration is briefly described in Chapter 5.

Under the Parochial Registers and Records Measure 1978, s. 6, the custody of the register books of the church rests with the churchwardens during a vacancy in the benefice, except that, where the right of presentation to the benefice is in suspense, and a priest-in-charge has been appointed, the priest-in-charge has the custody of them.

Before a new incumbent is appointed, the patron, if not himself the bishop, notifies to the bishop the name of the person whom he intends to present. In certain cases the patronage is vested in the parochial church council, and the election is then conducted by the churchwardens.

Before proceeding to institute or collate the successor, the bishop must send to the churchwardens by registered post a notice of his intention, together with particulars of the ecclesiastical preferments previously held by the clergyman in question, and a direction that the notice is to be fixed on the church door or notice-board for not less than one month, and then to be returned to the bishop with the churchwardens' certificate that the direction has been complied with.

(f) *Churchwardens as Bishops' Officers*

The churchwardens are the officers of the bishop, and it is their duty, on the bishop's or archdeacon's visitation at the end of their year of office, to answer such questions as may be put to them about the state of the parish and to report whatever may be amiss. They should also at any other time report to the bishop any irregularity or failure of duty of which he ought to be informed.

(3) ACTIONS BY AND AGAINST CHURCHWARDENS

Apart from any special statutory enactments, churchwardens are not a 'corporation' in the legal sense of having a corporate and continuous existence regardless of changes in the identity of the individual holders of the office; but they have certain attributes of a corporation. Thus they may hold church property, other than land, in perpetual succession, and in the City of London, they may hold land to the same purpose. In relation to any property so held, they can bring an action in their own names in respect of a matter which arose during the period of office of their predecessors, but they cannot be sued in respect of such a matter. Both churchwardens must concur in and be parties to the taking of legal proceedings.

Under modern law, contracts in relation to such matters as the supply of articles for use in the church, or repairs and additions to the fabric and other church property, are properly entered into, not by the churchwardens, but by the parochial church council. The council, therefore, is the proper body to sue or be sued on any such contracts.

9

Other Lay Officers

(1) Parish Clerk and Sexton—(2) Organist—(3) Verger—(4) Sidesmen—(5) Readers—(6) Deaconesses—(7) Lay Workers.

(1) PARISH CLERK AND SEXTON

By Section 7 (iii) of the Parochial Church Council (Powers) Measure 1956, the power to appoint and dismiss the parish clerk and sexton, or any person performing or assisting to perform the duties of parish clerk or sexton, and to determine their salaries and the conditions of the tenure of their offices or of their employment, is vested jointly in the parochial church council and the incumbent.

(2) ORGANIST

Under Canon B20 (as amended) an organist or choirmaster is appointed by the incumbent, with the agreement of the parochial church council. It is usually desirable that the terms of the appointment should be embodied in a written agreement. Termination of the appointment of an organist or choirmaster is likewise to be effected by the incumbent with the agreement of the council; but in exceptional circumstances the archdeacon (or, in the case of the archdeacon's own benefice, the bishop) may dispense with the need to obtain the council's agreement. The office of organist is not known to the common law and an organist as such has no legal status.

The organist, when appointed, is under the control of the incumbent, who is responsible for the music in church as part of the service, and may give directions as to the playing of the organ in the same way as he may with regard to the singing. But the incumbent is enjoined, by Canon B20, to pay due heed to the organist's advice and assistance in the choice of hymns, etc. and in the ordering of the music of the church.

(3) THE VERGER

The strict meaning of the title of verger is the official who carries a 'verge' or mace before a dignitary. In common usage the term denotes the official who takes care of the interior of the fabric of a church. He is the servant of the persons employing him, who should be the parochial church council. It is desirable that there should be a written contract containing the terms of the employment and the conditions on which it may be terminated by either side. The liability in case of an accident to the verger arising out of, or in the course of, his employment should be covered by insurance.

(4) SIDESMEN (AND WOMEN)

The annual parochial church meeting of a parish may (but is not obliged to) elect any number of sidesmen for the forthcoming year. The only qualification for a sidesman is that he or she should be on the electoral roll of the parish. The duty of sidesmen (and sideswomen), as stated in Canon E2, is to promote the cause of true religion in the parish and to assist the churchwardens in the discharge of their duties in maintaining order and decency in the church and churchyard, and especially during the time of divine service.

The practice of 'admitting' sidesmen and women at the same time as the churchwardens are admitted at the annual visitation has tended in recent years to fall into disuse, but is still observed in some places.

(5) READERS

Readers (often called 'lay readers') are lay officers of the Church whose functions include general pastoral and educational work, and in particular, as regards divine service, officiating at Morning and Evening Prayer (omitting the absolution), the publication of banns of marriage, the reading of the lessons, and preaching (see Canon E4).

Under Canon B12, a lay person may be specially authorised by the bishop, acting under such regulations as the General Synod may make from time to time, to distribute the sacrament of the Lord's Supper to the people. In practice a reader is frequently authorised under this power to administer the chalice at Holy Communion.

The use made by the Church of readers has considerably increased in recent years. They usually give their services voluntarily, but it is possible for a reader to be employed in a parish at a stipend.

Any person of either sex who is baptised and confirmed, and a regular communicant of the Church of England, is qualified to become a reader: but a candidate for the office must first undergo an examination of his or her knowledge and competence. A new reader, before being admitted to office, makes a declaration of assent, and that he or she will give due obedience to the bishop; the reader is then admitted by the bishop delivering to him or her the New Testament.

An admitted reader may not exercise his or her office in any diocese (except temporarily, with the bishop's written permission) unless he or she has been licensed to do so by the bishop of that diocese. Such licence may be revoked by the bishop at any time. There is a right of appeal to the archbishop against the revocation of a licence.

A register of admitted and licensed readers is kept in each diocese.

(6) DEACONESSES

The order of deaconesses is an order of women whose functions are the leading of public worship and pastoral care and instruction. It is described in Canon D1 as 'the one order of ministry in the Church of England to which women are admitted by prayer and the laying on of hands by the bishop'; but it is not one of the 'holy orders' of the Church, and deaconesses are members of the laity for all purposes.[1] They are normally employed in parochial work on a stipendiary basis. With the bishop's permission, and at the incumbent's invitation, a deaconess may say or sing Morning and Evening Prayer (save for the absolution), distribute the sacrament at the Holy Communion, and read the Epistle and Gospel. With the like permission and at the like invitation, she is also enabled (a) to preach at divine service; (b) to church women and, in the absence of the minister, to baptise; (c) with the goodwill of the persons responsible, to officiate at funerals; and (d) to publish banns of marriage at Morning or Evening Prayer.

A candidate for admission must be at least twenty-five years old, baptised, confirmed and a regular communicant of the Church of England; and she must undergo an examination of her religious knowledge. Before admission, she makes a declaration of assent, and swears an oath of obedience to the bishop.

A deaconess may not exercise her office in any diocese (except temporarily with the bishop's written permission) unless she has been licensed to do so by the bishop of that diocese.

[1] Under the Deacons (Ordination of Women) Measure 1986 it is now lawful for a woman to be ordained to the office of deacon and thus to be in holy orders. The status of the order of deaconesses remains unaffected by this Measure.

A register of admitted and licensed deaconesses is kept in each diocese.

(7) LAY WORKERS

Persons of either sex who have been admitted by the bishop as lay workers are employed in some parishes on a stipendiary basis. Before admitting a lay worker, the bishop must be satisfied that he is baptised, confirmed, and a regular communicant, and also that he has had the proper training and possesses the other neessary qualifications. A person who has been admitted to the office of Church Army evangelist is thereby admitted to be a lay worker.

An admitted lay worker may not serve as such in any diocese (except temporarily, with the bishop's written permission) unless he has been licensed to do so by the bishop of that diocese. Before being admitted or licensed he must make a declaration of assent, and that he will give due obedience to the bishop.

The functions of lay workers include (under the direction of the minister) the leading of public prayer, pastoral care, evangelisation, and instruction. With the bishop's permission and at the incumbent's invitation, a lay worker may say or sing Morning and Evening Prayer (save for the absolution), distribute the sacrament at the Holy Communion, and read the Epistle and Gospel. With the like permission and at the like invitation, he is also enabled (a) to preach at divine service; (b) to church women; (c) with the goodwill of the persons responsible, to officiate at funerals; and (d) to publish banns of marriage.

A register of admitted and licensed lay workers is kept in every diocese.

10

Parochial Church Meetings and Councils

(1) Introduction—(2) The Church Representation Rules (so far as relating to Parochial Church Meetings and Councils) with Notes—(3) The Parochial Church Councils (Powers) Measure 1956 (as Amended) with Notes—(4) Provisions of Pastoral Measure 1983 relating to Parochial Church Meetings and Councils in Special Cases, with Notes.

(1) INTRODUCTION

Previously to the Church of England Assembly (Powers) Act 1919,[1] the administration and finances of a parish were, in law, almost exclusively the prerogative of the incumbent and churchwardens. The general body of parishioners had little or no say in these matters, except in so far as they took part in the annual appointment of churchwardens. It is true that parochial church councils had been set up in most urban parishes, but they existed at the will of the incumbent and had no powers except such as he might delegate to them. Their existence was, however, some evidence both of the wishes of the laity to take a larger share of the burdens of parochial administration, and

[1] See p. 6 *ante*.

of the desire of the clergy to allow to the laity as a whole a voice in the affairs of the parish.

Parochial church councils were given a legal status for the first time by the Act of 1919, and by the Parochial Church Councils (Powers) Measure 1921, which was one of the first measures to be passed under the powers conferred by the Act. Rules as to the composition of parochial church councils, and as to the procedure in relation to meetings, were set out in a Schedule to the 'Constitution' of the Church Assembly appended to the Act, whilst the Measure defined the functions and powers of such councils.

At the present time, the composition and procedure of parochial church councils are regulated by the Church Representation Rules which constitute Schedule 3 (as since amended) to the Synodical Government Measure 1969, whilst their functions and powers are contained in the Parochial Church Councils (Powers) Measure 1956, as amended by the Measure of 1969. But in addition to the functions conferred by the Measure of 1956, parochial church councils also have a number of particular functions conferred by various other provisions, some of which are mentioned below.

The text of such parts of the Church Representation Rules as are relevant to parochial church councils, and the whole of the Parochial Church Councils (Powers) Measure 1956 (as amended), are set out in the pages which follow. But first, it may be of assistance to state briefly their general effect and the extent of the powers given to the laity in a parish.

The basis of the scheme is the electoral roll. This is a roll of persons who are qualified electors in a parish. They are lay persons of sixteen years of age or upwards, who are baptised and are members of the Church of England or of a Church in communion with the Church of England. They must also sign the form of application set out in an appendix to the Church Representation Rules. A person cannot be a qualified elector unless he resides in the parish, or is entered on the electoral roll as a non-resident elector. It is possible, however, for a person to be a qualified elector in any number of parishes at the same time, provided he satisfies the necessary conditions as regards each of them.

A non-resident elector, in addition to the qualifications other than residence required of electors who are resident in the parish, must for six months preceding the date of enrolment have habitually attended public worship in the parish on whose roll he seeks to be entered.

There is provision in the Rules for an annual revision of the electoral roll; also for the preparation of an entirely new roll in the year 1990, and thereafter in every succeeding sixth year.

The Rules provide for the holding, not later than the 30th April in each year, of an 'annual parochial church meeting' in which all those whose names are on the electoral roll of the parish are entitled to take part. This meeting elects lay members of the parochial church council; persons so elected must themselves be on the electoral roll of the parish and, as additional qualifications, they are required to be actual communicants and at least 17 years old. Other business which may be conducted at the same meeting consists of (i) the election (triennially) of lay representatives to the deanery synod, (ii) the election of sidesmen, (iii) the receiving of parochial and other reports, and (iv) the general discussion of church and parochial affairs. It is usual for this meeting to be held on the same day as and immediately after the 'meeting of the parishioners' for the appointment of churchwardens.

The incumbent or priest-in-charge is an *ex-officio* member and the *ex-officio* chairman of the parochial church council, which may also include other *ex-officio* members, and co-opted members, in addition to the elected members. The council is a body corporate with perpetual succession. It therefore has a legal existence apart from the members who compose it. To it have been transferred (amongst other powers) all the powers which, until the coming into force of the Parochial Church Councils (Powers) Measure 1921, were vested in the churchwardens in relation to (a) the financial affairs of the church, (b) the care, maintenance and insurance of the fabric of the church and its goods and ornaments, and (c) the care and maintenance of the churchyard.

The powers conferred on the council, as distinct from those transferred to it, include the power to acquire, manage and administer property for ecclesiastical purposes affecting the parish, power to frame an annual budget of moneys required for maintenance of church work, power to levy and collect a voluntary church rate for any church purpose, and power to make representations to the bishop with regard to any matter affecting the welfare of the church in the parish.

The council is also given power, jointly with the incumbent, to appoint and dismiss the parish clerk and sexton and to determine the salaries and conditions of service of these officers, and to determine the objects to which money collected in church are to be allocated.

All the powers so far mentioned are contained in the Parochial Church Councils (Powers) Measure 1956. There follow some examples of powers and functions conferred on parochial church councils by various other legislative provisions:

(i) A council is entitled to object to a proposal under the Parsonages Measure 1938 for the sale or pulling down of a residence house belonging to the benefice, or for the erection or purchase of a new residence house. Any such objection must be considered by the Church Commissioners before consenting to the proposal.

(ii) A parochial church council is given certain rights on the occurrence of a vacancy in the benefice by the Benefices (Exercise of Rights of Presentation)

Measure 1931; and in respect of a proposed transfer of the right of patronage by the Benefices (Transfer of Rights of Patronage) Measure 1930. These rights are considered in detail in Chapter 6 *ante*.

(iii) The council has an important voice in any decisions (a) as to the use of forms of service authorised by the Church of England (Worship and Doctrine) Measure 1974 and the canons made thereunder; (b) as to the use in Prayer Book services of any version of Scripture authorised by or under the Prayer Book (Versions of the Bible) Measure 1965; and (c) under Canon B8, as to any change of practice in regard to the vesture worn by a minister at divine service. These matters are dealt with at pp. 34 to 38 *ante*.

(iv) Under the Pastoral Measure 1983, the parochial church council of any parish which is liable to be affected by a proposed pastoral scheme or order is an 'interested party' whose views must be ascertained, and to whom an opportunity must be given of meeting the Pastoral Committee or a subcommittee or representative thereof. On the preparation of the draft scheme or order by the Church Commissioners, a copy of the draft must be sent to the council, together with a notice stating that written representations with respect to it must be made within a specified time, not being less than twenty-eight days.

(v) Under the Sharing of Church Buildings Act 1969, when the Church of England is concerned in a 'sharing agreement' relating to any church building, the parochial church council of the parish in which the building is situated is a necessary party to the agreement.

(vi) Where an incumbent or a vicar in a team ministry is subject to the age-limit provisions of the Ecclesiastical Offices (Age Limit) Measure 1975, the consent of the council is necessary to any extension of his tenure of office beyond the normal retiring age of 70.

(vii) Under the Incumbents (Vacation of Benefices Measure) 1977, a two-thirds majority of the lay members of a parochial church council may make a request for an inquiry under the Measure into the pastoral position in the parish (see p. 39 *ante*).

(viii) Under Canons F1 to F14, the parochial church council is charged with the provision of certain requisites of divine service. The articles so prescribed include a font, a holy table, communion plate, communion linen, surplices for the minister, a reading desk and a pulpit, seats for the congregation, church bells, a large Bible and Prayer Book and a pulpit Bible, an alms box, register books, and a service book and banns book. The council is also charged by the same canons with the general duty of the care and repair of all churches, chapels and churchyards within the parish.

With respect to team and group ministries established by pastoral schemes, and with respect also to new parishes created by pastoral schemes, and to cases where there are two or more parishes within the area of a single benefice or where two or more benefices are held in plurality, the Pastoral Measure 1983 contains special provisions relating to the parochial church meetings and councils of the parishes concerned. The text of these provisions is set out later in this Chapter.

(2) THE CHURCH REPRESENTATION RULES (SO FAR AS RELATING TO PAROCHIAL CHURCH MEETINGS AND COUNCILS) WITH NOTES[1]

PART I

CHURCH ELECTORAL ROLL

Formation of Roll

1. (1) There shall be a church electoral roll (in these rules referred to as 'the roll') in every parish, on which the names of lay persons shall be entered as hereinafter provided. The roll shall be available for inspection by bona fide inquirers.

(2) A lay person shall be entitled to have his name entered on the roll of a parish, if he[2]—

(*a*) is baptised;
(*b*) is a member of the Church of England or of a Church in communion with the Church of England:[3]
(*c*) is of sixteen years or upwards;[4]
(*d*) is resident in the parish, or, if not so resident, has habitually attended public worship in the parish during a period of six months prior to enrolment; and
(*e*) has signed the form of application for enrolment set out in section 1 of Appendix I to these rules.

[1] The Church Representation Rules in their original form were contained in Schedule 3 to the Synodical Government Measure 1969, but the Measure conferred a power to amend the Rules by resolution of the General Synod (a two-thirds majority being required in each House). The Rules were in fact so amended in 1973, 1980 and 1984. They relate not only to representation at the parish level but also to deanery and diocesan synods and the General Synod. The text (as amended) is here reproduced only of those rules which are relevant to representation at the parish level.

[2] Under the Interpretation Act 1978, words in the Rules importing the masculine gender include the feminine.

[3] Previously to these rules, membership of the Church of England was an essential qualification.

[4] Previously to the 1980 amendments of the Rules, the qualifying age was 17.

Provided that where a lay person will have his sixteenth birthday after the intended revision of the electoral roll or the preparation of a new roll but on or before the date of the annual parochial church meeting, he may complete a form of application for enrolment and his name shall be enrolled but with effect from the date of his birthday.

(3) A person shall be entitled to have his name on the roll of each of any number of parishes if he is entitled by virtue of paragraph (2) of this rule to have his name entered on each roll;[1] but a person whose name is entered on the roll of each of two or more parishes must choose one of those parishes for the purpose of the provisions of these rules which prescribe the qualifications for election to a deanery synod, a diocesan synod or the General Synod or for membership of a parochial church council under rule 12 (1) (e) or of a deanery synod under rule 19 (3) (b).[2]

[1] It is legally possible for a person to be 'resident' in two or more places at once, e.g. if he has a house in each place and regularly lives in each house for a substantial part of the year. Thus the qualification of being 'resident' may be satisfied simultaneously as regards each of the parishes in question. But see rule 44(6) (p. 128 *post*). Before the 1973 amendments of the rules, no person was allowed to be on the rolls of more than two parishes at the same time; but this limitation is now abolished.

[2] For the text of rule 12(1) (e) see p. 106 *post*. Under rule 19 (3) (b) (not set out *verbatim* in this book) a person who is on the roll of any parish in a particular deanery, and who is a lay member of the General Synod, or of the diocesan synod of the diocese to which the deanery belongs, is normally an *ex-officio* member of the deanery synod. The object of the latter part of this present rule 1(3) is to prevent any person who is on the rolls of two or more parishes (i) from being on that account eligible for election to the General Synod from more than one diocese (or from more than one electoral area within a diocese), or to any diocesan synod from more than one deanery, or to any deanery synod from more than one parish, or to more than one diocesan or deanery synod; (ii) if he is a member of the General Synod, or of a diocesan or deanery synod from being on that account an *ex-officio* member under rule 12 (1) (e), of more than one parochial church council; and (iii) if he is a member of the General Synod or of a diocesan synod, from being on that account an *ex-officio* member, under rule 19 (3) (b), of more than one deanery synod. For all these purposes, he must choose one of the parishes in question.

(4) The roll shall, until a parochial church council has been constituted in a parish, be formed and revised by the minister and churchwardens (if any), and shall, after such council has been constituted, be kept and revised by or under the direction of the council. Reference in this rule to a parochial church council shall, so far as may be necessary for giving effect to these rules, be construed as including references to the minister and churchwardens (if any).

(4A) Where a new parish is created by a pastoral scheme, the roll of that parish shall in the first instance consist—

(*a*) in the case of a parish created by the union of two or more former parishes, of the rolls of those parishes combined to form one roll;

(*b*) in any other case, of the names of the persons whose names are at the date of the coming into existence of the new parish entered on the roll of a parish the whole or any part of which forms part of the new parish and who are either resident in the new parish or have habitually attended public worship therein.[1]

(5) The parochial church council shall appoint a church electoral roll officer to act under its directions for the purpose of carrying out its functions with regard to the electoral roll.[2]

[1] Thus if a new parish is created, any existing electoral roll is to be used as the basis of the electoral roll of the new parish. Where the new parish is formed by the division of an existing parish, only those persons residing or worshipping in the area of the new parish are taken into account. Further names may, of course, be added to the roll in accordance with rule 1(6).

[2] Previously to these rules the appointment of an electoral roll officer was not an absolute legal requirement, though in practice many councils did appoint such an officer.

(6) The names of persons who are entitled to have their names entered upon the roll of the parish shall, subject to the provisions of these rules, be from time to time added to the roll. No name shall be added to or removed from the roll except by the authority of the parochial church council and it shall be the duty of that council to keep the roll constantly up to date and to cause names to be added and removed as from time to time required by these rules.

(7) Subject to the provisions of this rule, a person's name shall, as the occasion arises, be removed from the roll, if he:—

(*a*) has died; or

(*b*) becomes a clerk in Holy Orders; or

(*c*) signifies in writing his desire that his name should be removed; or

(*d*) ceases to reside in the parish, unless so ceasing he continues habitually to attend public worhsip in the parish, unless prevented from doing so by illness or other sufficient cause; or

(*e*) is not resident in the parish and has not attended public worship in the parish during the preceding six months, not having been prevented from doing so by illness or other sufficient cause; or

(*f*) was not entitled to have his name entered on the roll at the time when it was entered.

(8) The removal of a person's name from the roll under any of the provisions of these rules shall be without prejudice to his right to have his name entered again, if he has or acquires that right.

(9) The roll shall where practicable contain a record of the address of every person whose name is entered on the roll, but a failure to comply with this requirement shall not prejudice the validity of any entry on the roll.

Revision of Roll and Preparation of New Roll

2. (1) Except in a year in which a new roll is prepared, the roll of a parish shall be revised annually by or under the direction of the council. Notice of the intended revision in the form set out in section 2 of Appendix I to these rules shall be affixed by the minister or under his direction on or near the principal door of every church in the parish and every building in the parish licensed for public worship and remain so affixed for a period of not less than fourteen days before the commencement of the revision. The revision shall be completed not less than fifteen days or more than twenty-eight days before the annual parochial church meeting.

(2) Upon every revision all enrolments or removals from the roll which have been effected since the date of the last revision (or since the formation of the roll, if there has been no previous revision) shall be reviewed, and such further enrolments or removals from the roll as may be required shall be effected.

(3) After the completion of the revision, a copy of the roll as revised shall, together with a list of the names removed from the roll since the last revision (or since the formation of the roll, if there has been no previous revision), be published by being exhibited continuously for not less than fourteen days before the annual parochial church meeting on or near the principal door of the parish church in such manner as the council shall appoint. Subject to the proviso to rule 1(2),[1] no name shall be entered upon or removed from the roll during the period in any year between the completion of the revision and the close of the annual parochial church meeting.

[1] The name of a person whose sixteenth birthday falls between the revision of the roll and the date of the annual parochial church meeting may therefore be added to the roll during this period.

(4)[1] Not less than two months before the annual parochial church meeting in the year 1990 and every succeeding sixth year notice in the form set out in section 3 of Appendix 1 to these rules shall be affixed by the minister or under his direction on or near the principal door of every church in the parish and every building in the parish licensed for public worship and remain so affixed for a period of not less than fourteen days. On the affixing of the notice a new roll shall be prepared.

At every service held on each of the two Sundays within the period of fourteen days beginning with the date of the affixing of the notice or, in the case of a church in which no service is held on either of those Sundays, at every service held in that church on the first Sunday after that date the person conducting the service shall inform the congregation of the preparation of the new roll.

(5) The parochial church council shall take reasonable steps to inform every person whose name is entered on the previous roll that a new roll is being prepared and that if he wishes to have his name entered on the new roll he must apply for enrolment. No such steps need be taken with respect to any person whose name could be removed from the previous roll under rule 1(7).

(6) The new roll shall be prepared by entering upon it the names of persons entitled to entry under rule 1(2), and a fresh application shall be required from persons whose names were entered on the previous roll. A person whose name was so entered shall not be disqualified for entry on the new roll by reason only of his failure to comply with the

[1] Sub-paragraphs (4) to (7) provide for the preparation of an entirely new electoral roll in every parish in the year 1990, and in every succeeding sixth year. On every such occasion, every person whose name was entered on the previous roll must make a fresh application in order to be entered on the new roll. The requirement of a new roll at intervals of six years was imposed for the first time by these rules. Its object is to procure a periodical re-checking of every single name on the roll, and thus to ensure (as far as possible) the exclusion of all disqualified persons and of all persons who have ceased to take an active interest in Church affairs.

conditions specified in rule 1(2)(*d*), if he was prevented from doing so by illness or other sufficient cause, and the circumstances shall be stated on the application form. The preparation of the new roll shall be completed not less than fifteen days or more than twenty-eight days before the annual parochial church meeting.

(7) After the completion of the new roll, a copy shall be published by being exhibited continuously for not less than fourteen days before the annual parochial church meeting on or near the principal door of the parish church in such manner as the council shall appoint. No name shall be entered upon or removed from the roll during the period in any year between the completion of the new roll and the close of the annual parochial church meeting. On the publication of the new roll the previous roll shall cease to have effect.

(8) Upon the alteration of the boundaries of any parishes the parochial church council of the parish from which any area is transferred shall enquire from the persons resident in that area whose names are entered on the roll of the parish, whether they wish to have their names transferred to the roll of the other parish. The parochial church council shall remove the names of persons answering in the affirmative from its own roll and shall inform the parochial church council of the parish in which such persons now reside, which shall enter the names on its roll without any application for enrolment being required.

Procedural provisions relating to entry and removal of names

3. (1) When a person applying for enrolment on the roll of any parish signifies his desire that his name should be removed from the roll of any other parish, notice of that fact shall be sent by the parochial church council receiving the application to the parochial church council of that other parish.

(2) When the name of any person is removed from the roll of the parish owing to his having become resident in another parish, notice of that fact shall, whenever possible, be sent by the parochial church council of the first mentioned parish to the parochial church council of the last mentioned parish.

Certification of Numbers on Rolls[1]

4. (1) Not later than the first day of June—

(*a*) in any year immediately preceding a year in which elections of members of deanery synods or diocesan synods will fall due,

(*b*) in any year being the fourth year after the last preceding election of members of the House of Laity of the General Synod,

the number of names on the roll of each parish shall be certified to the secretary of the diocesan synod and the secretary of the deanery synod, and the certificate shall be signed by the chairman, vice-chairman, secretary or church electoral roll officer of the parochial church council:

Provided that, if the General Synod is at any time dissolved before the fourth year after the last preceding

[1] Rule 4 is necessary because the number of lay representatives elected by a parish to a deanery synod depends on the number of persons on the electoral roll of the parish: and similarly, the number of lay representatives elected by a deanery to a diocesan synod, or by a diocese to the General Synod, depends on the aggregate number of the names on the rolls of all the parishes in the deanery or the diocese (as the case may be). It is therefore necessary that the officials concerned with the elections to these respective synods should be furnished with the number of the names on the roll of each relevant parish, as on a date as near as practicable to the time of an election.

election of the House of Laity or before this rule has taken effect during that year, the General Synod or the Presidents thereof may give directions requiring the number of names on the roll of each parish to be certified as aforesaid within such time as may be specified, and the directions may, if the dissolution is known to be impending, be given before it occurs.

(2) A copy of such certificate shall be fixed at or near to the principal door of every church in the parish and every building licensed for public worship in the parish when the certificate is sent to the secretary of the diocesan synod, and shall remain so affixed for a period of not less than fourteen days.

(3) Any question as to the accuracy of any certificate given under this rule shall be decided in such manner as the diocesan synod or the bishop's council and standing committee shall determine.

Provision with respect to Person whose Name is on Guild Church Roll.

4A. (1) A person whose name is entered on the roll of a guild church shall for the purpose of the provisions of these rules which prescribe the qualifications for election to a deanery synod, a diocesan synod or the House of Laity of the General Synod, or for membership of a deanery synod under rule 19(3)(b), be deemed to be a person whose name is on the roll of the parish in which the guild church is, and references in those provisions or in rule 1(3) to a person whose name is on the roll of a parish or on the roll of each of two or more parishes, and in rule 37 to entry on the roll of a parish, shall be construed accordingly.

(2) In this rule 'guild church' means a church in the City of London designated and established as a guild church

under the City of London (Guild Churches) Acts 1952 and 1960.[1]

PART II

PAROCHIAL CHURCH MEETINGS AND COUNCILS ANNUAL MEETINGS

Annual Meetings

5. (1) In every parish there shall be held not later than the 30th April in each year[2] the annual parochial church meeting (hereafter in these rules referred to as 'the annual meeting').

(2) All lay persons whose names are entered on the roll of the parish shall be entitled to attend the annual meeting and to take part in its proceedings, and no other lay person shall be so entitled.[3]

[1] As to guild churches generally, see pp. 28 and 29 *ante*. The object of this rule (added in 1973) is to put any person who is on the roll of a guild church in the same position, as regards eligibility for election to or membership of any synod, as if he were on the roll of the parish in which the guild church is situated. For the text of rule 1(3) and the effect of rule 19(3)(b) (not set out *verbatim* in this book) see p. 88 *ante*. Rule 37 (also not set out *verbatim*) provides in effect (*inter alia*) that if an elected member of the House of Laity of the General Synod ceases either to be entered on the roll of any parish in the diocese for which he was elected, or to be a habitual worshipper at any cathedral church in the diocese, his seat shall be vacated, unless the bishop's council and standing committee of the diocese otherwise determine.

[2] Previously to these rules, the meeting had to be held 'not later in the year than the week following Easter week'.

[3] The rules do not expressly lay down whether members of the general public are entitled to be admitted to the meeting to observe the proceedings, and it is thought that the meeting itself can resolve either to admit or to exclude them. Where, as is frequently the arrangement, the meeting immediately follows the meeting of parishioners for the appointment of churchwardens, lay persons who are entitled to attend the meeting of parishioners, but who are not on the electoral roll, should be called upon either (if the public are not being admitted) to leave at the end of the meeting of parishioners, or (if the public are being admitted) to remain, if they so desire, as observers only.

(3) A clerk in Holy Orders shall be entitled to attend the annual meeting of a parish and take part in its proceedings—

(*a*) if he is either beneficed in or licensed to the parish or any other parish in the area of the benefice to which the parish belongs; or

(*b*) if he is resident in the parish and is not beneficed in or licensed to any other parish;[1] or

(*c*) if he is not resident in the parish and is not beneficed or licensed to any other parish, the parochial church council with the concurrence of the minister has declared him to be a habitual worshipper in the parish, such declaration being effective until the conclusion of the annual meeting in the year in which a new roll is prepared under rule 2 or his ceasing to be a habitual worshipper in the parish whichever it the earlier, but without prejudice to a renewal of such declaration; or

(*d*) if he is a co-opted member of the parochial church council in accordance with rule 12(1)(g).

(4) Without prejudice to paragraphs (2) and (3) of this rule—

(*a*) all the members of the team of a team ministry shall be entitled to attend, and take part in the proceedings of, the annual meeting of the parish or each of the parishes in the area of the benefice for which the team ministry is established, and where the area of a group ministry includes the area of a benefice for which a

[1] Section 45 of the Cathedrals Measure 1963 provides that residentiary and minor canons of a parish church cathedral may attend the annual parochial church meeting of the parish of that cathedral, whether or not they are resident in the parish. This section is not expressly repealed, and it would seem that the clergy in question still have this right, even though, if not resident in the parish, they do not come within any of the categories specified in this rule.

team ministry is established, all the vicars in that ministry shall be entitled to attend, and take part in the proceedings of, the annual meeting of each of the other parishes in the area for which the group ministry is established;

(*b*) all the incumbents and priests in charge in a group ministry shall be entitled to attend and take part in the proceedings of the annual meeting of each of the parishes in the area for which the group ministry is established.

(5) Where two or more benefices are held in plurality and a team ministry is, or is to be, established for the area of one of those benefices, then, if a pastoral scheme provides for extending the operation of the team ministry, so long as the plurality continues, to the area of any other benefice so held, paragraph (4) of this rule shall have effect as if the references to the area of the benefice were references to the combined area of the benefices concerned.

Convening of Meeting

6. (1) The annual meeting shall be convened by the minister of the parish by a notice in the form set out in section 4 of Appendix 1 to these rules affixed on or near to the principal door of every church in the parish and every building licensed for public worship in the parish, for a period including the last two Sundays before the day of the meeting.

(2) The annual meeting shall be held at such place on such date and at such hour as shall be directed by the previous annual meeting, or by the parochial church council (which may vary any direction given by a previous annual meeting) or in the absence of any such direction as shall be appointed by the minister.

(3) During the vacancy of the benefice or curacy or when the minister is absent or incapacitated by illness or any

other cause, the vice-chairman of the parochial church council, or if there is no vice-chairman, or if he is unable or unwilling to act, the secretary of or some other person appointed by that council shall have all the powers vested in the minister under this rule.

(4) The annual meeting shall be held at a place within the parish unless the parochial church council decide otherwise.

(5) The minister of a new parish created by a pastoral scheme, or, in the absence of the minister, a person appointed by the bishop, shall as soon as possible after the scheme comes into operation convene a special parochial church meeting, and, subject to paragraph (6) of this rule, the provisions of these rules relating to the convening and conduct of the annual meeting shall apply to a special meeting convened under this paragraph.

(6) A special meeting so convened and held in the month of November or the month of December may, if the meeting so resolves, be for all purposes under these rules the annual meeting for the succeeding year, and a special meeting to convened shall in any event be for all such purposes the annual meeting for the year in which it is so convened and held.

Chairman

7. (1) The minister, if present, or if he is not present, the vice-chairman of the parochial church council, or, if he also is not present, a chairman chosen by the annual meeting shall preside thereat.

(2) Where a parish is in the area of a benefice for which a team ministry is established, and a vicar in that ministry is entitled to preside at an annual meeting of that parish by virtue of a provision in a pastoral scheme or the bishop's licence assigning to the vicar the duties, or a share in the duties, of the chairmanship of the annual meeting of that

parish, then, if both he and the vice-chairman of the parochial church council are not present at that meeting, but the rector in that ministry is present, the rector shall preside thereat.

(3) In the case of an equal division of votes, the chairman shall have a second or casting vote, unless it is a case where rule 10(8) applies; but no clerical chairman shall have a vote in the election of the parochial representatives of the laity.[1]

Business

8. (1) The annual meeting shall receive from the parochial church council and shall be free to discuss:—

(*a*) a copy or copies of the roll;
(*b*) an annual report on the proceedings of the parochial church council;
(*c*) an annual report on the financial affairs of the parish;
(*d*) the audited accounts of the parochial church council for the year ending on the 31st December immediately preceding the meeting;
(*e*) an audited statement of the funds and property, if any, remaining in the hands of the parochial church council at the said date;
(*f*) a report upon the fabric, goods and ornaments of the church or churches of the parish; and
(*g*) a report on the proceedings of the deanery synod.

(2) The council shall cause a copy of the said audited accounts and the said audited statement to be affixed on or

[1] Previously to these rules, a clerical chairman was permitted a casting vote in an election though not an original vote, but now the casting vote is also disallowed and where there is an equality of votes the decision is by lot; see rule 10(8) *post*. That the spin of a coin should be preferred to the wisdom of the presiding cleric may be thought a somewhat extreme application of the principle of excluding all clerical influence in the election of lay representatives.

near the principal door of every church in the parish and every building licensed for public worship in the parish at least seven days before the annual meeting.

(3) Such accounts and statement shall be submitted to the annual meeting for approval. If approved, they shall be signed by the chairman of the meeting, who shall then deliver them to the parochial church council for publication, and the parochial church council shall forthwith cause them to be published and affixed for a period of at least fourteen days on or near the principal door of every church in the parish and every building licensed for public worship in the parish and at such other conspicuous place or places in the parish as the parochial church council think appropriate and shall cause a copy to be sent to the secretary of the diocesan board of finance.

(4) The annual meeting shall in the manner provided by rule 10 of these rules:—

(*a*) elect in every third year parochial representatives of the laity to the deanery synod;
(*b*) elect parochial representatives of the laity to the parochial church council;
(*c*) elect sidesmen;[1]

and the elections shall be carried out in the above order.

(5) The annual meeting shall appoint the auditors to the council.

(6) Without prejudice to the foregoing provisions and rule 6(6), a special parochial church meeting convened under rule 6(5) shall, in addition to other business:—

(*a*) decide on the number of members of the parochial

[1] The election of sidesmen is in fact optional. Under the rules previously in force, the sidesmen (if any) were elected by the annual meeting and the minister; and if the meeting and the minister could not agree, half were elected by the meeting and the other half appointed by the minister. Now all are elected by the meeting and the minister is excluded from any vote.

church council who are to be elected representatives of the laity;

(*b*) elect in the manner provided by rule 10 parochial representatives of the laity to the deanery synod, if such representatives are required to be elected in the year for which that meeting is the annual meeting by virtue of rule 6(6).

(7) Any person entitled to attend the annual meeting may ask any question about parochial church matters, or bring about a discussion of any matter of parochial or general church interest, by moving a general resolution or by moving to give any particular recommendation to the council in relation to its duties.

(8) The annual meeting shall have power to adjourn and to determine its own rules of procedure.

(9) The secretary of the parochial church council (or another person appointed by the meeting in his place) shall act as a clerk of the annual meeting, and shall record the minutes thereof.

Qualifications of persons to be chosen or elected by annual meetings

9. (1) Subject to the provisions of rule 1(3), the qualifications of a person to be elected a parochial representative of the laity to either of the bodies referred to in the last preceding rule[1] are that—

(*a*) his name is entered on the roll of the parish; and

(*b*) he is an actual communicant member of the Church of England or, in the case of election to the parochial church council, an actual communicant member of any Church in communion with the Church of England; and

(*c*) in the case of election to the parochial church council,

[1] i.e. the deanery synod and the parochial church council.

he is of seventeen years or upwards, and in the case of election to the deanery synod, he is of eighteen years or upwards;

Provided that the registrar of the diocese shall not be qualified for election to any of the said bodies in that diocese.

(1A) Notwithstanding paragraph (1) hereof, a baptised person who—

(*a*) is of communicant status in another Church which subscribes to the doctrine of the Holy Trinity; and
(*b*) is in good standing in that Church; and
(*c*) is an habitual worshipper and a communicant at the parish church or at some other building licensed for public worship in the parish; and
(*d*) is of seventeen years and upwards,

may, with the prior permission of the bishop, be nominated for election as a parochial representative of the laity to the parochial church council.

Provided that at least two-thirds of the parochial representatives of the laity to the parochial church council shall have the qualifications set out in paragraph (1) hereof.

(2) The qualification of a person to be elected a sidesman is that his name is entered on the roll of the parish.

(3) No person shall be elected under the last preceding rule unless he has signified his consent to serve or there is in the opinion of the meeting sufficient evidence of his willingness to serve.

Conduct of Elections at Annual Meetings

10. (1) Subject to the provisions of any scheme made under Rule 10A and for the time being in force this rule shall apply to all elections at annual meetings.

(2) All candidates for elections at an annual meeting must be nominated and seconded by persons entitled to attend the annual meeting, and in the case of parochial

representatives of the laity, by persons whose names are entered on the roll of the parish. A candidate shall be nominated or seconded either before the meeting in writing or at the meeting.

(3) If the number of candidates nominated is not greater than the number of seats to be filled, the candidates nominated shall forthwith be declared elected.

(4) If more candidates are nominated than there are seats to be filled, the election shall take place at the annual meeting.

(5) No clerk in Holy Orders shall be entitled to vote in the election of any parochial representative of the laity.[1]

(6) Each person entitled to vote shall have as many votes as there are seats to be filled but may not give more than one vote to any one candidate.

(7) Votes may be given:—

(*a*) on voting papers, which must be signed by the voter on the reverse thereof; or

(*b*) if no person present objects thereto, by show of hands.

(8) Where owing to an equality of votes an election is not decided the decision between the persons for whom the equal numbers of votes have been cast shall be taken by lot.

(9) The result of any election by an annual meeting shall be announced as soon as practicable by the person presiding over the election, and a notice of the result shall in every case be affixed on or near the principal door of every church in the parish and every building licensed for public worship in the parish, and shall bear the date on which the result is declared. The notice shall remain affixed for not less than fourteen days.

(10) Returns of parochial representatives of the laity elected to the deanery synod shall be sent to the secretary of that synod.

[1] Previously to these rules, a clerical chairman had a casting though not an original vote.

Variation of Method of Election by Scheme

10A. (1) The annual meeting may make a scheme which provides that the election of parochial representatives of the laity to the parochial church council or to the deanery synod or to both that council and that synod shall be conducted by the method of the single transferable vote under rules, with the necessary modifications, made by the General Synod under rule 33(4) and for the time being in force.[1]

(2) No scheme under this rule shall be valid unless approved by at least two-thirds of the persons present and voting at the annual meeting nor shall it be operative until the next ensuing annual meeting. Every such scheme shall, on its approval, be communicated to the bishops' council and standing committee of the diocesan synod which shall consider the scheme, determine whether or not the scheme shall come into operation and inform the secretary of the parochial church council of its decision.

CONDUCT OF ELECTIONS OF CHURCHWARDENS

11. (1) If elections of churchwardens take place at meetings of parishioners under section 3 of the Churchwardens

[1] Rule 33(4), as amended, not printed *verbatim* in this book, provides for the making of rules by the General Synod for elections by the single transferable vote system, which rules apply to elections to the General Synod itself. In 1980, by the introduction of Rule 10A, it was made optional for the annual meeting of any parish to make provision for the election of representatives of the parish to the deanery synod, and of members of the parochial church council, by proportional representation. In 1984 Rule 10A was amended to substitute the method of the single transferable vote for proportional representation. Under this system, each voter indicates in order of preference the candidates whom he supports. When the votes are counted the surplus first preference votes are redistributed in accordance with the second choice on those voting papers. The process is repeated until sufficient candidates each have a majority. Whether the annual meetings of many or any parishes will avail themselves of this option is questionable.

(Appointment and Resignation) Measure 1964[1] either because there has been no joint consent under section 2 of that Measure or because there is no minister, the elections shall be conducted, announced and notified in the same manner as elections under rule 10, except that all persons entitled to attend the meeting of parishioners other than the minister shall be entitled to nominate and vote at such elections of churchwardens.

(2) . . . .[2]

PAROCHIAL CHURCH COUNCIL

Members

12. (1) Subject to the provisions of rule 1 (3) the parochial church council shall consist of:—

(*a*) all clerks in Holy Orders beneficed in or licensed to the parish;
(*b*) any deaconess or lay worker licensed to the parish;
(*bb*) in the case of a parish in the area of a benefice for which a team ministry is established, all the members of the team of that ministry;
(*c*) the churchwardens, being actual communicant members of the Church of England whose names are on the roll of the parish;
(*d*) such, if any, of the readers whose names are on the roll of the parish, as the annual meeting may determine;
(*e*) all persons whose names are on the roll of the parish and who are lay members of any deanery synod, diocesan synod or the General Synod;
(*f*) such number of representatives of the laity as the

[1] See p. 60 *et seq, ante* for the text of this Measure and notes thereto. The amendments effected by these rules are there indicated by appropriate alterations of the text and by explanatory notes.

[2] Rule 11(2) amends the Churchwardens (Apppointment and Resignation) Measure 1964; the text of the measure is printed in chapter 7 as amended by the rule.

annual meeting may decide, and so that the number determined may be altered from time to time by a resolution passed at any annual meeting, but such resolution shall not take effect before the next ensuing annual meeting; and

(*g*) co-opted members, if the parochial church council so decides, not exceeding in number one-fifth of the representatives of the laity elected under the last preceding sub-paragraph of this paragraph, and being either clerks in Holy Orders or actual lay communicant members of the Church of England of seventeen years of age or upwards. The term of office of a co-opted member shall be until the conclusion of the next annual meeting; but without prejudice to his being co-opted on subsequent occasions for a similar term, subject to and in accordance with the provisions of these rules.

(1A) Any person chosen, appointed or elected as a churchwarden of a parish, being an actual communicant member of the Church of England whose name is on the roll of the parish, shall as from the date on which the choice, appointment or election, as the case may be, is made be a member of the parochial church council of the parish by virtue of this paragraph until he is admitted to the office of churchwarden, and he shall thereafter continue to be a member of that council by virtue of sub-paragraph (c) of paragraph (1) of this rule unless and until he ceases to be qualified for membership by virtue of that sub-paragraph.[1]

[1] Under this provision, introduced in 1980, a newly chosen, appointed or elected churchwarden having the necessary qualifications, although he does not take office as churchwarden until admitted as such, will at once become a member of the parochial church council. After having been admitted as churchwarden, unless in the meantime he has become disqualified, he will continue an *ex-officio* member of the council until the admission as churchwarden of his successor in office.

(2) If:—

(*a*) the name of any person, being an elected representative of the laity, is removed from the roll of the parish under rule 1, or

(*b*) any such person refuses or fails to apply for enrolment when a new roll for a parish is being prepared,

that person shall cease to be a member of the parochial church council of the parish on the date on which his name is removed from the roll or, as the case may be, on the date on which the new roll is completed, but the preceding provisions are without prejudice to any right which the council may have to make that person a co-opted member.

(3) Where a group ministry is established the incumbents of all benefices in the group, every priest in charge of any benefice therein and where the area of the group ministry includes the area of a benefice for which a team ministry is established, all the vicars in that ministry shall be entitled to attend meetings of the parochial church councils of all the parishes in the area for which the group ministry is established. They shall be entitled to receive documents circulated to members of councils of which they are not themselves members and to speak but not to vote at meetings of such councils.

(4) Where two or more benefices are held in plurality and a team ministry is, or is to be, established for the area of one of those benefices, then, if a pastoral scheme provides for extending the operation of the team ministry, so long as the plurality continues, to the area of any other benefice so held, paragraphs (1)(bb) and (3) of this rule shall have effect as if the references to the area of the benefice were references to the combined area of the benefices concerned.

General Provisions relating to Parochial Church Councils

13. The provisions in Appendix II to these rules shall have effect with respect to parochial church councils, and with respect to the officers, the meetings and the proceedings thereof:

Provided that a parochial church council may, with the consent of the diocesan synod, vary the said provisions, in their application to the council.

Term of office

14. (1) Representatives of the laity on the parochial church council of a parish shall hold office from the conclusion of the annual meeting until the conclusion of the next annual meeting of the parish:

Provided that the annual meeting may decide that one-third only (or the number nearest to one-third) of the representatives of the laity elected to the council shall retire from office in every year. In any case where it is so decided, the representatives of the laity to retire from office at each annual meeting shall be those who have been longest in office since last elected,[1] and as between representatives of the laity elected on the same day, those to retire shall (unless they otherwise agree among themselves) be selected by lot. A representative of the laity shall in any event retire at the conclusion of the third annual meeting after that at which he was elected.

(2) Persons who are members of a parochial church council by virtue of their election as lay members of a deanery synod shall hold office for a term beginning with

[1] This provision takes effect subject to rule 39(9) under which, when a person has been elected to fill a casual vacancy, he holds office only for the unexpired portion of the term of office of the person in whose place he was elected (see p. 122 *post*).

the date of their election and ending with the 31st May next following the election of their successors.[1]

Limitations on years of service

15. The annual meeting may decide that no representative of the laity on the parochial church council may hold office for more than a specified number of years continuously and may also decide that after a specified interval a person who has ceased to be eligible by reason of such decision may again stand for election as a representative of the laity on the council.[2]

Parishes with more than one Place of Worship

16. (1) In any parish where there are two or more churches of places of worship the annual meeting may make a scheme, which makes provision for either or both of the following purposes, that is to say:—

(*a*) for the election of the representatives of the laity to the parochial church council in such manner as to ensure due representation of the congregation of each such church or place; and

(*b*) for the election by the annual meeting for any district

[1] The reason for this rule is that an elected member of the deanery synod continues to be a member thereof down to and including the 31st May in the year in which new elections are held, and it is deemed expedient that so long as he is such a member, he should remain on the parochial church council. It should, however, be noted that if, at the relevant annual meeting, a sitting member of the deanery synod is not re-elected to that synod, the fact that his *ex-officio* membership of the parochial church council is prolonged till the ensuing 31st May is no bar to his election as an ordinary member of the council, for the normal term, at the same annual meeting.

[2] This power is newly conferred by these rules.

in the parish in which a church or place of worship is situated of a district church council for that district.[1]

(2) A scheme for the election of any district church council or councils under the preceding paragraph shall provide for the election of representatives of the laity on to such council, for *ex-officio* members and for the chairmanship of such council and shall contain such other provisions as to membership and procedure as shall be considered appropriate by the annual meeting.

(3) Such a scheme may also provide for the delegation by the parochial church council to a district church council of such functions as it may specify and subject to the scheme the parochial church council may delegate to a district church council such of its functions as it shall think fit but not including (in either case) the functions of a parochial church council as interested parties under Part 1 of the Pastoral Measure 1983.

(4) A scheme may provide for the election or choice of one or two deputy churchwardens, and for the delegation to him or them of such functions of the churchwardens relating to any church or place as the scheme may specify, and the churchwardens may, subject to the scheme, delegate such of their said functions as they think fit to the deputy churchwarden or churchwardens.

(5) No scheme under this rule shall be valid unless approved by at least two-thirds of the persons present and voting at the annual meeting nor shall the scheme provide for it to come into operation until such date as the bishop's council and standing committee may determine being a date not later than the next ensuing annual meeting. Every such scheme shall on its approval be communicated to the bishop's council and standing committee of the diocesan synod which may determine—

[1] The power to establish 'district church councils' with or without 'deputy churchwardens', otherwise than in the case of team ministries, is newly conferred by these rules.

(*a*) that the scheme shall come into operation; or
(*b*) that the scheme shall not come into operation; or
(*c*) that the scheme shall come into operation with specified amendments, if such amendments are approved by an annual or special parochial church meeting and the scheme as amended is approved by at least two-thirds of the persons present and voting at that meeting.

(6) Where a pastoral scheme establishing a team ministry, or an instrument of the bishop made by virtue of that scheme[1], makes, in relation to a parish in the area of the benefice for which the team ministry is established, any provision which may be made by a scheme under this rule, no scheme under this rule relating to that parish shall provide for the scheme to come into operation until on or after the date on which the provisions in question of the pastoral scheme or of the instrument, as the case may be, cease to have effect.

(7) A scheme under this rule may be varied or revoked by a subsequent scheme thereunder.

(8) Every member of the team of a team ministry shall have a right to attend the meetings of any district church council elected for any district in a parish in the area of the benefice for which the team ministry is established.

(9) This rule shall be without prejudice to the appointment, in parishes with more than one parish church, of two churchwardens for each church under section 27(5) of the Pastoral Measure 1983.[2]

(10) In this rule 'place of worship' means a building or part of a building licensed for public worship.

[1] See Schedule 3, paragraph 4 of the Pastoral Measure 1983, printed at p. 152 *post*, and p. 116 footnote *post*.

[2] Section 27(5) of the Pastoral Measure 1983 provides that where a parish has more than one parish church, two churchwardens shall be appointed for each of the parish churches, and that the Churchwardens (Appointment and Resignation) Measure 1984 shall apply separately to each pair of churchwardens. All churchwardens are however to be churchwardens of the whole parish, except so far as they arrange to perform separate duties in relation to the parish churches within it.

Joint Parochial Church Councils

17. (1) Where there are two or more parishes within the area of a single benefice or two or more benefices are held in plurality, the annual meetings of all or some of the parishes in the benefice or benefices may make a joint scheme to provide—

(*a*) for establishing a joint parochial church council (hereinafter referred to as 'the joint council') comprising the ministers of the parishes and such numbers of representatives of each of those parishes elected by and from among the other members of the parochial church council of the parish as may be specified in the scheme;

(*b*) for the chairmanship, meetings and procedure of the joint council;

(*c*) for the delegation by the parochial church council of each such parish to the joint council of such of its functions, other than its functions as an interested party under Part I of the Pastoral Measure 1983 as may be so specified.[1]

(2) Subject to the scheme and to any pastoral scheme or order made under paragraph 13 of Schedule 3 to the said Measure, the parochial church council of any such parish may delegate to the joint council such of its functions, other than its functions as an interested party under the said Part I, as it thinks fit.

(3) The joint council shall meet from time to time for the purpose of consulting together on matters of common concern.

(4) No scheme under this rule shall be valid unless approved by at least two-thirds of the persons present and voting at the annual meeting nor shall the scheme provide for it to come into operation until such date as the bishop's council and standing committee may determine being a

[1] See p. 21 *ante* for the position of interested parties.

date not later than the next ensuing annual meeting. Every such scheme shall on its approval be communicated to the bishop's council and standing committee of the diocesan synod which may determine—

(*a*) that the scheme shall come into operation; or
(*b*) that the scheme shall not come into operation; or
(*c*) that the scheme shall come into operation with specified amendments, if such amendments are approved by an annual or special parochial church meeting and the scheme as amended is approved by at least two-thirds of the persons present and voting at that meeting.

(5) A special parochial church meeting of a parish to which this rule applies may be convened for the purpose of deciding whether to join in making such a scheme, and where such a meeting is convened the foregoing provisions shall have effect with the substitution for references to the annual meeting of references to the special meeting.

(6) Where a pastoral scheme or order, or any instrument of the bishop made by virtue of such a scheme or order,[1] establishes a joint parochial church council for two or more of the parishes in a single benefice or two or more of the parishes in benefices held in plurality, no scheme under this rule relating to those parishes shall provide for the scheme to come into operation until on or after the date on which the provisions of the pastoral scheme, pastoral order or instrument, as the case may be, establishing the joint parochial church council cease to have effect.

(7) Where provisions of a pastoral scheme or order for the holding of benefices in plurality are terminated under section 18(2) of the Pastoral Measure 1983 any provision of a scheme under this rule establishing a joint parochial

[1] The requirements of such a scheme or order are outlined in Schedule 3, paragraph 13 of the Pastoral Measure 1983, printed at p. 156 *post*. Since the arrangements made under a pastoral scheme or order have a maximum duration of five years, a scheme made under rule 17 would normally be needed to replace those arrangements when they expired.

church council for all or some of the parishes of those benefices and the other provisions thereof affecting that council shall cease to have effect on the date on which the first mentioned provisions cease to have effect.

(8) A scheme under this rule may be varied or revoked by a subsequent scheme thereunder.

Team Councils

17A. (1) Where a team ministry is established for the area of a benefice which comprises more than one parish the annual meetings of the parishes in that area may make a joint scheme to provide—

(*a*) for establishing a team council comprising—
  (i) all the members of the team;
  (ii) every assistant curate, deaconess and lay worker licensed to any such parish; and
  (iii) such number of lay representatives elected by and from among the lay representatives of the parochial church council of each parish in the area as may be specified in the scheme;

(*b*) for the chairmanship, meetings and procedure of the team council; and

(*c*) for the delegation by the parochial church council of each such parish to the team council of such functions, other than its functions as an interested party under Part I of the Pastoral Measure 1983.[1]

(2) Subject to the scheme and to any pastoral scheme relating to the team council made under paragraph 3(7) of Schedule 3 to the said Measure, the parochial church council of any such parish may delegate to the team council such of its functions, other than its functions as an interested party under the said Part I, as it thinks fit.

[1] See p. 21 *ante* for the position of interested parties.

(3) The team council shall meet from time to time for the purpose of consulting together on matters of common concern.

(4) No scheme under this rule shall be valid unless approved by at least two-thirds of the persons present and voting at the annual meeting nor shall the scheme provide for it to come into operation until such date as the bishop's council and standing committee may determine being a date not later than the next ensuing annual meeting. Every such scheme shall on its approval be communicated to the bishop's council and standing committee of the diocesan synod which may determine—

(*a*) that the scheme shall come into operation; or
(*b*) that the scheme shall not come into operation; or
(*c*) that the scheme shall come into operation with specified amendments, if such amendments are approved by an annual or special parochial church meeting and the scheme as amended is approved by at least two-thirds of the persons present and voting at that meeting.

(5) A special parochial church meeting of a parish to which this rule applies may be convened for the purpose of deciding whether to join in making such a scheme, and where such a meeting is convened the foregoing provisions shall have effect with the substitution for references to the annual meeting of references to the special meeting.

(6) Where a pastoral scheme establishing a team ministry, or an instrument of the bishop made by virtue of that scheme,[1] establishes a team council for that ministry, no scheme under this rule relating to that ministry shall provide for the scheme to come into operation until on or after the date on which the provisions of the pastoral scheme or

[1] The requirements of such a scheme or order are outlined in Schedule 3, paragraph 4 of the Pastoral Measure 1983, printed at p. 152 *post*. Since the arrangements made under a pastoral scheme or order have a maximum duration of five years, a scheme made under rule 17A would normally be needed to replace those arrangements when they expired.

of the instrument, as the case may be, establishing the team council cease to have effect.

(7) A scheme under this rule may be varied or revoked by a subsequent scheme thereunder.

Group Councils

17B. (1) Where a pastoral scheme establishes a group ministry, the annual meetings of the parishes in the area for which the group ministry is established may make a joint scheme to provide—

(*a*) for establishing a group council comprising—
   (i) all the members of the group ministry,
   (ii) every assistant curate, deaconess, and lay worker licensed to any such parish, and
   (iii) such number of lay representatives elected by and from among the lay members of the parochial church council of each such parish, as may be specified in the scheme;

(*b*) for the chairmanship, meetings and procedure of the group council; and

(*c*) for the delegation by the parochial church council of each such parish to the group council of such functions, other than its functions as an interested party under Part I of the Pastoral Measure 1983,[1] as may be so specified.

(2) If the area of a group ministry includes the area of a benefice for which a team ministry is established, a scheme under this rule shall provide for the vicars in that ministry, as well as the rector, and all the other members of the team to be members of the group council.

(3) Paragraphs (2) to (7) of rule 17A shall apply in relation to a scheme under this rule as they apply in relation to a scheme under that rule with the modification that for the

[1] See p. 21 *ante* for the position of interested parties.

references to a team ministry and a team council there shall be substituted references to a group ministry and a group council respectively.

SPECIAL AND EXTRAORDINARY MEETINGS

18. (1) In addition to the annual meeting, the minister of a parish may convene a special parochial church meeting, and he shall do so on a written representation by not less than one-third of the lay members of the parochial church council; and the provisions of these rules relating to the convening and conduct of the annual meeting shall, with the necessary modifications, apply to a special parochial church meeting.

(2) On a written representation made to the archdeacon by not less than one-third of the lay members of the parochial church council, or by one-tenth of the persons whose names are on the roll of the parish, and deemed by the archdeacon to have been made with sufficient cause, the archdeacon shall convene an extraordinary meeting of the parochial church council or an extraordinary parochial church meeting, and shall either take the chair himself or shall appoint a chairman to preside. The chairman, not being otherwise entitled to attend such meeting, shall not be entitled to vote upon any resolution before the meeting.

(3) In any case where the archdeacon is himself the minister, any representation under paragraph (2) of this rule shall be made to the bishop, and in any such case the references to the archdeacon in paragraph (2) of this rule shall be construed as references to the bishop, or to a person appointed by him to act on his behalf.

(4) All lay persons whose names are entered on the roll of the parish on the day which is twenty-one clear days before the date on which any special or extraordinary parochial church meeting is to be held shall be entitled to attend the meeting and to take part in its proceedings, and no other lay person shall be so entitled.

(5) A clerk in Holy Orders shall be entitled to attend any such meeting and to take part in its proceedings if by virtue of rule 5(3), (4) or (5) he would have been entitled to attend the annual meeting of the parish had it been held on the same date, and no other such clerk shall be so entitled.

PARTS III, IV AND V . . .[1]

PART VI
APPEALS AND DISQUALIFICATIONS

Appeals

36. (1) There shall be a right of appeal by any person aggrieved against:—

(*a*) any enrolment, or refusal of enrolment, on the roll of a parish;
(*b*) the removal of any name, or the refusal to remove any name, from the roll of a parish;
(*c*) the allowance or disallowance of any vote given or tendered in an election of a churchwarden or in an election under these rules or to a body constituted under or in accordance with these rules;
(*d*) the result of any election of a churchwarden or of any election or choice held or made or purporting to be held or made under these rules, or any election or choice of members of a body constituted under or in accordance with these rules.

(2) In the case of an appeal arising out of an election to the House of Laity of the General Synod or the diocesan synod or the choosing of a retired clerk in Holy Orders in

[1] Parts III, IV, and V of the rules (comprising rules 19 to 35) relate exclusively to deanery synods, diocesan synods and the General Synod, and are here omitted.

accordance with rule 19(2)(e)[1] notice of the appeal shall be given in writing to the bishop. In any other case, notice of the appeal shall be given in writing to the lay chairman of the deanery synod. Notices under this paragraph shall be given:—

(*a*) in the case of an appeal against an enrolment or a refusal of an enrolment, or in the case of an appeal against the removal of any name or the refusal to remove any name from the roll, not later than fourteen days after the date of the enrolment, removal or refusal or, if the appeal arises on the revision of the roll or the preparation of a new roll, not later than fourteen days after the first publication of the revised or new roll under rule 2(3) or (7);

(*b*) in the case of an appeal against the allowance or disallowance of a vote, not later than fourteen days after such allowance or disallowance;

(*c*) in the case of an appeal against the result of an election, not later than fourteen days after the result thereof has been announced by the presiding officer.

(3) An error in the electoral roll shall not be a ground of appeal against the result of any election unless—

(i) either it has been determined under this rule that there has been such an error or the question is awaiting determination under this rule; and

(ii) the error would or might be material to the result of the election;

and the allowance or disallowance of a vote shall not be a ground of appeal against the result of an election unless the allowance or disallowance would or might be material to the result of the election.

[1] The cases referred to in the first sentence of rule 36(2) relate exclusively to elections to synods. At the parochial level, notice is to be given to the lay chairman of the deanery synod, who proceeds in accordance with rule 36(5) (*post*).

(4) . . .[1]

(5) In any appeal arising under this rule except an appeal arising out of an election to the House of Laity of the General Synod, the bishop or the lay chairman of the deanery synod,[2] as the case may be, shall, unless the parties agree to a settlement of their dispute, refer any appeal to the bishop's council and standing committee of the diocese who, in an appeal concerning an election of the House of Clergy of the diocesan synod, shall appoint three or a greater number being an odd number of their clerical members to consider and decide the appeal and, in an appeal concerning lay persons, the bishop's council and standing committee shall appoint three or a greater number, being an odd number of their lay members to consider and decide the appeal. Their decision shall be final.

(6) For the purpose of the consideration and decision of any appeal under this rule, the members of the standing committee or bishop's council, as the case may be, shall consider all the relevant circumstances, and shall be entitled to inspect all documents and papers relating to the subject matter of the appeal, and be furnished with all information respecting the same which they may require. They shall give to the parties to the appeal an opportunity of appearing before them in person or through a legal or other representative.

(7) The members of the standing committee or bishop's council, as the case may be, shall have power at any time to extend the time within which a notice of appeal is given.

37. . . .[3]

[1] Rule 36(4) relates exclusively to the General Synod, and is here omitted.

[2] Only the lay chairman of the deanery synod is concerned with parochial appeals; see rule 36(2), *ante*.

[3] Rule 37 relates exclusively to vacation of membership of a deanery or diocesan synod or of the General Synod, and is here omitted.

Ex-officio Membership not to Disqualify for Election

38. No person shall be disqualified from being elected or chosen a member of any body under these rules by the fact that he is also a member *ex-officio* of that body; and no person shall be deemed to vacate his seat as such an elected or chosen member of any body by reason only of the fact that subsequently to his election or choice he has become a member of that body *ex-officio.*

Part VII

SUPPLEMENTARY AND INTERPRETATION

Casual Vacancies

39.[1] (1) Where a casual vacancy among the parochial representatives elected to the parochial church council or deanery synod occurs, the vacancy may be filled by the election by the parochial church council of a person qualified to be so elected.

(2) . . .

(3) Subject to paragraphs (1), (2) and (6) of this rule, casual vacancies among persons elected under these rules shall be filled by elections conducted in the same manner as ordinary elections.

(4) Elections to fill casual vacancies shall, where possible, be held at such times as will enable all casual vacancies among representatives of the laity who are electors to be filled at the time of every election to the House of Laity of the General Synod, but no such election shall be invalid by reason of any casual vacancies not having been so filled.

(5) Elections to fill casual vacancies shall be held as soon as reasonably practicable after the vacancy has occurred....

(6) and (7) . . .

[1] So much of this rule as is not relevant to elections at the parochial level has been omitted.

(8) The preceding provisions of this rule shall apply, so far as applicable and with the necessary modifications, to the choosing of persons under these rules as it applies to the election of persons thereunder, and shall also apply to the election or choosing of members of any body constituted under or in accordance with these rules.

(9) Any person elected or chosen to fill a casual vacancy shall hold office only for the unexpired portion of the term of office of the person in whose place he is elected or chosen.

Resignations

40. Any person holding any office under these rules or being a member of any body constituted by or under these rules may resign his office or membership by notice in writing signed by him and sent or given to the secretary of the body of which he is an officer or member, as the case may be; and his resignation shall take effect on the date specified in the notice or, if no date is so specified, on the receipt of the notice by the secretary of that body.

Notices

41. Any notice or other document required or authorised to be sent or given under these rules shall be deemed to have been duly sent or given if sent through the post addressed to the person to whom it is required or authorised to be sent or given at that person's last known address.

Revocation and Variation of Rules, etc.

42. Subject to the provisions of these rules any power conferred by these rules to make, approve, frame, pass or adopt any rule, order, resolution, determination, decision, appointment or scheme, or to give any consent or settle any constitution, or to prescribe the manner of doing anything, shall be construed as including a power, exercisable in a like manner and subject to the like conditions, to revoke or vary any such rule, order, resolution, determination, decision, appointment, scheme, consent or constitution, or anything so prescribed.

Special Provisions

43. (1) In the carrying out of these rules in any diocese the bishop of such diocese shall have power:—

(*a*) to make provisions for any matter not herein provided for;

(*b*) to appoint a person to do any act in respect of which there has been any neglect or default on the part of any person or body charged with any duty under these rules;

(*c*) so far as may be necessary for the purpose of giving effect to the intention of these rules, to extend or alter the time for holding any meeting or election or to modify the procedure laid down by these rules in connection therewith provided that such power shall not be exercised in relation to the conduct of the elections referred to in rule 39 of these rules;[1]

(*d*) in any case in which there has been no valid election, to direct a fresh election to be held and to give such directions in connection therewith as he may think necessary; and

(*e*) in any case in which any difficulties arise, to give any directions which he may consider expedient for the purpose of removing the difficulties.

(2) The powers of the bishop under this rule shall not enable him:—

[1] Thus where there is a casual vacancy the procedure laid down in rule 39 *ante* must be followed.

(*a*) to validate anythying that was invalid at the time when it was done;

(*b*) to give any direction that is contrary to any resolution of the General Synod.

(3) No proceedings of any body constituted under these rules shall be invalidated by any vacancy in the membership of that body or by any defect in the qualification, election or appointment of any members thereof.

(4) No proceedings shall be invalidated by the use of a form which differs from that prescribed by these rules if the form which has in fact been used is to a substantially similar effect. Any question as to whether the form which has been used is to a substantially similar effect shall be determined by the bishop.

(5) In the case of an omission in any parish to prepare or maintain a roll or form or maintain a council or to hold the annual meeting, the rural dean upon such omission being brought to his notice shall ascertain and report to the bishop the cause thereof.

(6) During a vacancy in an archbishopric or where by reason of illness an archbishop is unable to exercise his functions under these rules or to appoint a commissary under paragraph (10) of this rule the functions of an archbishop under these rules shall be exercisable by the other archbishop.

(7) During a vacancy in a diocesan bishopric the functions of a diocesan bishop under these rules, including his functions as president of the diocesan synod, shall be exercisable by such person, being a person in episcopal orders, as the archbishop of the province may appoint.

(8) Where by reason of illness a diocesan bishop is unable to exercise his functions under these rules or to appoint a commissary under paragraph (10) of this rule, the archbishop of the province may, if he thinks it necessary or expedient to do so, appoint a person in episcopal orders to exercise the functions mentioned in paragraph (7) of this rule during the period of the bishop's illness.

(9) If a person appointed in pursuance of paragraph (7) or (8) of this rule becomes unable by reason of illness to act under the appointment, the archbishop may revoke the appointment and make a fresh one.

(10) An archbishop or diocesan bishop may appoint a commissary and delegate to him all or any of the functions of the archbishop or bishop under these rules, but if a bishop proposes to delegate to a commissary his functions as one of the authorities which together constitute the diocesan synod he shall appoint a person in episcopal orders as commissary.

(11) If a person appointed in pursuance of paragraph (7) or (8) of this rule, or a person to whom the functions of president of the diocesan synod are delegated under paragraph (10) hereof, is a member of the house of clergy of the diocesan synod, his membership of that house shall be suspended during the period for which the appointment or delegation has effect.

Meaning of Minister, Parish and other words and phrases

44. (1) In these rules:—

'actual communicant member of the Church of England' means a member of the Church of England who is confirmed or ready and desirous of being confirmed and has received Communion according to the use of the Church of England or of a Church in communion with the Church of England at least three times during the twelve months preceding the date of his election or appointment;

'actual communicant member of a Church in communion with the Church of England' means a communicant member of a Church in communion with the Church of England who has received Communion according to the use of the Church of England or of a Church in communion with the Church of England at least three times during the twelve months preceding the date of his election or appointment;

'the Measure' means the Synodical Government Measure 1969:

'minister' means:—

(*a*) the incumbent of a parish;
(*b*) a curate licensed to the charge of a parish or a minister acting as priest-in-charge of a parish in respect of which rights of presentation are suspended; and
(*c*) a vicar in a team ministry to the extent that the duties of a minister are assigned to him by a scheme under the Pastoral Measure 1968[1] or his licence from the bishop;

'parish' means:—

(*a*) an ecclesiastical parish; and
(*b*) a district which is constituted a 'conventional' district for the cure of souls.

'public worship' means public worship according to the rites and ceremonies of the Church of England.

(2) Any reference in these rules to the laity shall be construed as a reference to persons other than clerks in Holy Orders, and the expresion 'lay' in these rules shall be construed accordingly.

(3) Where a person has executed a deed of relinquishment under the Clerical Disabilities Act 1870 and the deed has been enrolled in the High Court and recorded in the registry of a diocese under that Act then, unless and until the vacation of the enrolment of the deed is recorded in such a registry under the Clerical Disabilities Act 1870 (Amendment) Measure 1934, that person shall be deemed not to be a clerk in Holy Orders for the purpose of para-

[1] Now the Pastoral Measure 1983.

graph (2) above or of any other provision of these rules which refers to such a clerk.[1]

(4) References in these rules to the cathedral church of the diocese shall include, in the case of the dioceses of London and Oxford, references to Westminster Abbey and St. George's Chapel, Windsor, respectively.

(5) If any question arises whether a Church is a Church in communion with the Church of England, it shall be conclusively determined for the purposes of these rules by the Archbishops of Canterbury and York.

(6) In these rules words importing residence include residence of a regular nature but do not include residence of a casual nature.

(7) Any reference herein to 'these rules' shall be construed as including a reference to the Appendices hereto.

[1] Under the Act of 1870 referred to in the text, it is possible for an ordained minister of the Church of England, subject to certain conditions, to execute a deed of relinquishment whereby, upon the enrolment of the deed in the High Court and its being recorded in the registry of the appropriate diocese, the minister in question becomes incapable of officiating as such, and is at the same time freed from all disabilities and disqualifications to which an ordained minister is normally subject by law. The Measure of 1934, also referred to in the text, provides a procedure whereby, on the petition of the minister concerned, the enrolment of the deed of relinquishment can be vacated, and upon its vacation being recorded in the diocesan registry, the minister will revert to the same status as he had before the execution, enrolment and recording of the deed. The object of this present sub-rule (3) (introduced in 1980) is to make it clear beyond doubt that an ordained minister who has availed himself to the Act of 1870 is to be regarded as a member of the laity for all the purposes of the Rules (e.g. entry on an electoral roll, voting rights, and election as a layman to a synod or parochial church council) unless and until he reverts to his former status under the procedure provided by the Measure of 1934.

APPENDIX 1

Section 1

Rule 1(2)

APPLICATION FOR ENROLMENT ON CHURCH ELECTORAL ROLL

I ....

(Full Christian name and surname)

of ....

(Full postal address)

am baptised and am a member of the Church of England or of a Church in communion with it. I am sixteen years or over and am either resident in the parish or a habitual attender at public worship there for at least the past six months.

I apply for entry on the church electoral roll of the parish of

....

Signed ....

Date................................

NOTES

1. The only Churches at present in communion with the Church of England are other Anglican Churches and certain foreign Churches. Members of other Churches in England are usually admitted to communion as individuals, but their Churches are not yet in communion with the Church of England. Such persons would naturally take part in the government of their own Churches.

2. Every six years a new roll is prepared and those on the previous roll are informed so that they can re-apply. If you are not resident in the parish but were on the roll as an habitual worshipper and have been prevented by sickness or absence or other essential reason from worshipping for the past six months, you may write 'would' before 'have habitually attended' in the form and add 'but was prevented from doing so because . . .' and then state the reason.

3. If you have any problems over this form, please approach the clergy or lay people responsible for the parish, who will be pleased to help you.

4. In this Form 'parish' means an ecclesiastical parish.

Section 2

Rule 2(1)

FORM OF NOTICE OF REVISION OF CHURCH ELECTORAL ROLL

Diocese of...

Parish of ....

Notice is hereby given that the Church Electoral Roll of the above parish will be revised by the Parochial Church Council,* beginning on

.... the ....day of.. 19........ and ending

on .... the .... day of .... 19........

After such Revision, a copy of the Roll will forthwith be exhibited on, or near to, the principal door of the Parish Church for inspection.

Under the Church Representation Rules any persons are entitled to have their names entered on the roll, if they:—

(i) are baptised,
(ii) are members of the Church of England or of any Church in communion with the Church of England.
(iii) are sixteen or over,
(iv) are resident in the parish, or, not being resident in the parish, have habitually attended public worship in the parish during the six months before the date of application for enrolment, and
(v) have signed a form of application for enrolment.

Forms of application for enrolment can be obtained from the undersigned, and should be returned, if possible, in time for the Revision.

Any error discovered in the Roll should at once be reported to the undersigned.

Dated this†.............................. day of.. 19.......

....

Church Electoral Roll Officer

Address ....

NOTE—In this Notice 'parish' means an ecclesiastical parish.

*The revision must be completed not less than 15 days or more than 28 days before the Annual Parochial Church Meeting.

†Not less than 14 days notice must be given.

Section 3

Rule 2(1)

FORM OF NOTICE OF PREPARATION OF NEW ROLL

Diocese of..

Parish of ....

Notice is hereby given that under the Church Representation Rules a new Church Electoral Roll* is being prepared. All persons who wish to have their names entered on the new Roll, whether their names are entered on the present Roll or not, are requested to apply for enrolment if possible not later than..

....

The new roll will come into operation on...

....

Forms of application for enrolment can be obtained from the undersigned.

Under the Church Representation Rules any persons are entitled to have their names entered on the Roll, if they:—

(i) are baptised,
(ii) are members of the Church of England or of any Church in communion with the Church of England,
(iii) are sixteen or over,
(iv) are resident in the parish, or, not being resident in the parish, have habitually attended public worship in the parish during the six months before the date of application for enrolment, and
(v) have signed a form of application for enrolment.

Any error discovered on the Roll should at once be reported to the undersigned.

Dated this.. day of .... 19........

....
Church Electoral Roll Officer

Address ....

NOTE—In this Notice 'parish' means an ecclesiastical parish.
*The new roll must be completed not less than 15 days or more than 28 days before the Annual Parochial Church Meeting.

Section 4

Rule 6(1)

NOTICE OF ANNUAL PAROCHIAL CHURCH MEETING

Parish of ....

The Annual Parochial Church Meeting will be held in ....

....

on .... day of .... at ....

For the election of Parochial representatives of the laity as follows:—

*To the Deanery Synod ....representatives.

To the Parochial Church Council .... representatives.

For the election of Sidesmen.

For the consideration of:—

(*a*) A copy or copies of the Roll;
(*b*) An Annual Report on the proceedings of the Council;
(*c*) An Annual Report on the financial affairs of the parish;
(*d*) The audited Accounts of the Council for the year ending on the 31st December immediately preceding the meeting;
(*e*) An audited Statement of the funds and property of the Council;
(*f*) A Report upon the fabric, goods and ornaments of the church or churches of the parish;
(*g*) A Report on the proceedings of the Deanery Synod;

and other matters of parochial or general Church interest.

All persons whose names are entered upon the Church Electoral Roll of the parish (and such persons only) are entitled to vote at the election of parochial representatives of the laity.

A person is qualified to be elected a parochial representative of the laity to the deanery synod if:—

(*a*) his name is entered on the church electoral roll of the parish;
(*b*) he is a member of the Church of England who is confirmed or ready and desirous of being confirmed and has received Communion according to the use of the Church of England or a Church in communion with the Church of England at least three times during the twelve months preceding the date of the election; and
(*c*) he is of 18 years or upwards.

*Include where applicable.

A person is qualified to be elected a parochial representative of the laity to the parochial church council if:—

(*a*) his name is entered on the church electoral roll of the parish; and
(*b*) he is a member of the Church of England who is confirmed or ready and desirous of being confirmed or a communicant member of a Church in communion with the Church of England and has received Communion according to the use of the Church of England or a Church in communion with the Church of England at least three times during the twelve months preceding the date of the election; and
(*c*) he is of 17 years or upwards.

Any person whose name is on the roll may be a sidesman.

Signed .... †Minister of the parish.

† Or 'Vice-Chairman of the Parochial Church Council' as the case may be (see rule 6(3) of the Church Representation Rules).

The remaining Sections of this Appendix relate only to diocesan synods and are here omitted.

APPENDIX 2 Rule 13

GENERAL PROVISIONS RELATING TO PAROCHIAL CHURCH COUNCILS

Officers of the council.

1.—(*a*) The minister of the parish shall be chairman of the parochial church council (hereinafter referred to as 'the council').

(*b*) A lay member of the council shall be elected as vice-chairman of the council.

(*c*) During the vacancy of the benefice or when the chairman is incapacitated by absence or illness or any other cause or when the minister invites him to do so the vice-chairman of the council shall act as chairman and have all the powers vested in the chairman.

(*d*) The council may appoint one of their number to act as secretary of the council. If no member is appointed so to act the council shall appoint some other fit person with such remuneration (if any) as they shall think fit. The secretary shall have charge of all documents relating to the current business of the council except that, unless he is the electoral roll officer, he shall not have charge of the roll. He shall be responsible for keeping the minutes, shall record all resolutions passed by the council and shall keep the secretary of the diocesan synod and deanery synod informed as to his name and address.

(*e*) The council may appoint one or more of their number to act as treasurer solely or jointly. Failing such appointment, the office of treasurer shall be discharged jointly by such of the churchwardens as are members of the council, or, if there is only one such churchwarden, by the churchwarden solely. No remuneration shall be paid to any person in respect of his appointment as treasurer.

(*f*) The council shall appoint an electoral roll officer, who may but need not be a member of the council and may be the secretary, and if he is not a member may pay to him such remuneration as it shall think fit. He shall have charge of the roll.

(*g*) If auditors to the council are not appointed by the annual meeting, or if auditors appointed by the annual meeting are unable or unwilling to act, auditors (who shall not be members of the council) shall be appointed by the council. The remuneration (if any) of the auditors shall be paid by the council.

Meetings of council.

2. The council shall hold not less than four meetings in each year. Meetings shall be convened by the chairman and if not more than four meetings are held they shall be at quarterly intervals so far as possible.

Power to call meetings.

3. The chairman may at any time convene a meeting of

the council. If he refuses or neglects to do so within seven days after a requisition for that purpose signed by not less than one-third of the members of the council has been presented to him those members may forthwith convene a meeting.

Notices relating to meetings.

4.—(*a*) Except as provided in paragraph 8 of this Appendix, at least ten clear days before any meeting of the council notice thereof specifying the time and place of the intended meeting and signed by or on behalf of the chairman of the council or the persons convening the meeting shall be posted at or near the principal door of every church, or building licensed for public worship in the parish.

(*b*) Not less than seven days before the meeting a notice thereof specifying the time and place of the meeting signed by or on behalf of the secretary shall be sent to every member of the council. Such notice shall contain the agenda of the meeting including any motion or other business proposed by any member of the council of which notice has been received by the secretary.

(*c*) If for some good and sufficient reason the chairman, vice-chairman and secretary, or any two of them, consider that a convened meeting should be postponed, notice shall be given to every member of the council specifying a reconvened time and place within fourteen days of the postponed meeting.

Chairman at meetings.

5. Subject to the provisions of rule 18 the chair at a meeting of the council shall be taken:—

(*a*) by the chairman of the council if he is present;
(*b*) if the chairman of the council is not present, or his

office is vacant, by the vice-chairman of the council if he is present;

(*c*) in the case of a parish in the area of a benefice for which a team ministry is established, by the rector in that ministry if he is present and both the vicar in that ministry who would if he were present be entitled, by virtue of a provision in a pastoral scheme or the bishop's licence, to preside and the vice-chairman of the council are not present.

Provided that at any such meeting the chairman presiding shall, if he thinks it expedient to do so or the meeting so resolves, vacate the chair either generally or for the purposes of any business in which he has a personal interest or for any other particular business.

Should neither the chairman or vice-chairman nor, where sub-paragraph (c) above applies, the rector be available to take the chair for any meeting or for any particular item on the agenda during a meeting then a chairman shall be chosen by those members present from among their number and the person so chosen shall preside for that meeting or for that particular item.

Quorum and agenda.

6. No business shall be transacted at any meeting of the council unless at least one-third of the members are present thereat and no business which is not specified in the agenda shall be transacted at any meeting except by the consent of three-quarters of the members present at the meeting.

Order of business.

7. The business of a meeting of the council shall be transacted in the order set forth in the agenda unless the council by resolution otherwise determine.

Short notice for emergency meetings.

8. In case of sudden emergency or other special circumstances requiring immediate action by the council a meeting may be convened by the chairman of the council at not less than three clear days' notice in writing to the members of the council but the quorum for the transaction of any business at such meetings shall be a majority of the then existing members of the council and no business shall be transacted at such meeting except as is specified in the notice convening the meeting.

Place of meetings.

9. The meeting of the council shall be held at such place as the council may direct or in the absence of such direction as the chairman may direct.

Vote of majority to decide.

10. The business of the Council shall be decided by a majority of the members present and voting thereon.

Casting vote.

11. In the case of an equal division of votes the chairman of the meeting shall have a second or casting vote.

Minutes.

12.—(*a*) The names of the members present at any meeting of the council shall be recorded in the minutes.

(*b*) If one-fifth of the members present and voting on any resolution so require, the minutes shall record the names of the members voting for and against that resolution.

(*c*) Any member of the council shall be entitled to require that the minutes shall contain a record of the manner in which his vote was cast on any resolution.

(*d*) Members of the council shall have access to the minutes of all meetings, but no other person, other than the bishop or the archdeacon or a person authorised by either of them in writing, shall have access to the minutes or part thereof without the authority of the council.

Adjournments.

13. Any meeting of the council may adjourn its proceedings to such time and place as may be determined at such meeting.

Standing committee.

14.—(*a*) The council shall have a standing committee consisting of not less than five persons. The minister and such of the churchwardens as are members of the council shall be *ex-officio* members of the standing committee, and the council shall by resolution appoint at least two other members of the standing committee from among its own members and may remove any person so appointed.

(*b*) The standing committee shall have power to transact the business of the council between the meetings thereof subject to any directions given by the council.

Other committees.

15. The council may appoint other committees for the purpose of the various branches of church work in the parish, and may include therein persons who are not members of the council. The minister shall be a member of all committees *ex-officio.*

Validity of proceedings.

16. No proceedings of the council shall be invalidated by any vacancy in the membership of the council or by any

defect in the qualification or election of any member thereof.

Interpretation.

17. Any question arising on the interpretation of this Appendix shall be referred to the bishop of the diocese and any decision given by him or by any person appointed by him on his behalf shall be final.[1]

(3) THE PAROCHIAL CHURCH COUNCILS (POWERS) MEASURE 1956 (AS AMENDED) WITH NOTES

A Measure to consolidate with amendments certain enactments relating to parochial church councils and parochial charities (5th July, 1956).

Definitions.

1. In this Measure—

'Council' means a parochial church council;

'Diocesan Authority' means the Diocesan Board of Finance or any existing or future body appointed by the Diocesan Conference[2] to act as trustees of diocesan trust property;

'Minister' and 'Parish' have the meanings respectively assigned to them in the Rules for the Representation of the Laity;[3]

'Relevant date' means the first day of July, 1921.[4]

[1] It has been held that this provision does not oust the jurisdiction of the ordinary courts on a question of interpretation.

[2] The predecessor of the Diocesan Synod.

[3] These rules have been replaced by the Church Representation Rules. The relevant definitions are now contained in rule 44 of the last-mentioned rules (p. 126 *ante*).

[4] The date of the coming into force of the original Parochial Church Councils (Powers) Measure 1921, which this Measure has replaced.

General functions of council.

2.[1] (1) It shall be the duty of the minister and the parochial church council to consult together on matters of general concern and importance to the parish.

(2) The functions of parochial church councils shall include—

(*a*) co-operation with the minister in promoting in the parish the whole mission of the Church, pastoral, evangelistic, social and ecumenical;[2]

(*b*) the consideration and discussion of matters concerning the Church of England or any other matters of religious of public interest, but not the declaration of the doctrine of the Church on any question;

(*c*) making known and putting into effect any provision made by the diocesan synod or the deanery synod, but without prejudice to the powers of the council on any particular matter;

(*d*) giving advice to the diocesan synod and the deanery synod on any matter referred to the council;

(*e*) raising such matters as the council consider appropriate with the diocesan synod or deanery synod.

[1] This section was substituted by the Synodical Government Measure 1969 for the original section 2, which read: 'It shall be the primary duty of the council in every parish to co-operate with the minister in the initiation, conduct and development of church work both within the parish and outside.' The new section, in accordance with the general scheme of synodical government, lays greater emphasis on the part to be played by the laity.

[2] It is permissible for the council to apply a reasonable part of its general funds for any purposes which will further 'the whole mission of the Church' as so described, e.g. by subscriptions to charities. Having regard in particular to the word 'social', it is considered that subscriptions may properly be made to charities for the relief of sick, poor or other necessitous persons, even though the objects of such charities are not specifically religious.

(3) In the exercise of its functions the parochial church council shall take into consideration any expression of opinion by any parochial church meeting.

Council to be a body corporate.

3. Every council shall be a body corporate by the name of the parochial church council of the parish for which it is appointed and shall have perpetual succession.[1] Any act of the council may be signified by an instrument executed pursuant to a resolution of the council and under the hands or if an instrument under seal is required under the hands and seals of the chairman presiding and two other members of the council present at the meeting at which such resolution is passed.

Powers vested in council as successor to certain other bodies.

4. (1) Subject to the provisions of any Act or Measure passed after the relevant date and to anything lawfully done under such provisions, the council of every parish shall have—

(i) The like powers duties and liabilities as immediately before the relevant date, the vestry[2] of such parish had

[1] These words give the council a corporate existence independent of the personnel comprised in it. It is a separate entity recognised by law, and exists as such for all time.

[2] The vestry was a parochial body which included the incumbent or curate-in-charge, and the persons of both sexes who were rated for the relief of the poor in respect of the parish, whether resident therein or not, and the occupiers of heraditaments so rated. It originally had both civil and ecclesiastical functions, but it was deprived of practically all its civil functions by statute many years ago. Immediately before the coming into force of the Parochial Church Council (Powers) Measure 1921, its principal ecclesiastical functions were the election of churchwardens and the other matters specified (whether as included in or as excluded from the transfer of functions to the council) in this present paragraph (i).

with respect to the affairs of the church except as regards the election of churchwardens and sidesmen[1] and as regards the administration of ecclesiastical charities[2] but including the power of presentation to the benefice of such parish if the right to present thereto was vested in or in trust for the parishioners and the power of making any voluntary church rate.[3]

(ii) The like powers duties and liabilities as, immediately before the relevant date, the churchwardens of such parish had with respect to—

[1] As to the modern law relating to the appointment of churchwardens, see Chapter 7 *ante*. As to the election of sidesmen by the annual parochial church meeting, see p. 101 *ante*.

[2] Broadly speaking, this expression covers every charity for the religious purposes of any church or denomination. The administration of any such charity which was originally vested in the vestry remains so vested unless it has been transferred to some other persons or body by a scheme made by the court or the Charity Commissioners.

[3] The right to enforce or compel the payment of a church rate in any ecclesiastical or other court was taken away by the Compulsory Church Rates Abolition Act 1868; but the same Act expressly reserved the power for vestries, in both ancient and modern parishes and districts, to make and assess a church rate, on the footing that payment by the person on whom it is assesed is voluntary. A 'church rate' is defined for this purpose as a rate for ecclesiastical purposes, i.e. for the 'building, rebuilding, enlargement and repair of any church or chapel, and any purpose to which by common or ecclesiastical law a church rate is applicable, or any of such purposes.'

The Act did not affect the recovery of church rates specially imposed by any private or local Act of Parliament, where the power to levy the rate was conferred for valuable consideration (such as the extinguishment of tithes or customary payments) of a nature specified in the Act. Such rates are still enforceable.

In practice, the power conferred by the Act to make a voluntary church rate was never of much value in most parishes, and its use at the present day is rare. But for what it is worth it is now vested in the parochial church council. When it is proposed to exercise it, it would appear that it is the duty of the churchwardens to prepare an estimate of the sum required and to lay it before the council, in the same way as they formerly prepared such an estimate and laid it before the vestry. After the churchwardens have done this they are relieved of responsibility.

(*a*) The financial affairs of the Church including the collection and administration of all moneys raised for church purposes and the keeping of accounts in relation to such affairs and moneys;[1]

(*b*) The care maintenance preservation and insurance of the fabric of the church and the goods and ornaments thereof;[2]

(*c*) The care and maintenance of the churchyard (open or closed), and the power of giving a certificate under the provisions of section eighteen of the Burial Act, 1855, with the like powers as immediately before the relevant date were possessed by the churchwardens to recover the cost of maintaining a closed churchyard.[3]

[1] As to money collected in church, see section 7(iv) *post*, and note thereto.

[2] There is no *duty* to insure except a moral one. The general duty of repair now extends to the chancel when the incumbent is rector, by virtue of section 52 of the Ecclesiastical Dilapidations Measure 1923. A *lay* rector remains personally liable for the repair of the chancel, except in those cases (probably the majority) where the liability has been voluntarily compounded under the provisions of the Act of 1923, or has been extinguished under the terms of the Tithe Act 1936.

[3] A churchyard may be 'closed', i.e. discontinued for burials, by an Order in Council made under the Burial Acts. Under section 18 of the Burial Act 1855, a procedure was established for transferring the duty of maintaining a churchyard so closed in decent order, and its walls and fences repaired, from the churchwardens (or latterly the parochial church council) to the local authority. Except in the City of London where it still applies, this procedure is now superseded by the Local Government Act 1972, section 215. Under the last-mentioned section, if a churchyard has been closed by Order in Council, the parochial church council may serve a written request on the appropriate local authority to take over its maintenance, and the liability for maintenance passes from the parochial church council to the local authority three months after such service. In the case of a churchyard within a civil parish, the notice should be served on the parish council or, if there is no parish council, on the chairman of the parish meeting; and in any other case, it should be served on the district council or London borough council in whose area the churchyard is situated. But when the notice is served on a parish council or the chairman of a parish meeting, the parish council or meeting may, by passing an appropriate resolution and by giving written notice thereof both to the parochial church council and to the district council before the

Provided that nothing herein contained shall affect the property[1] of the churchwardens in the goods and ornaments of the church or their powers duties and liabilities with respect to visitations.[2]

(iii) The like powers duties and liabilities as, immediately before the relevant date, were possessed by the church trustees[3] (if any) for the parish appointed under the Compulsory Church Rate Abolition Act, 1868.

(2) All enactments in any Act whether general or local

expiration of the three months' period, transfer its liability to the district council. In order to avoid inconvenience to local authorities, however, parochial church councils are urged to give informal notice twelve months before they wish the local authority to assume responsibility; but it would be wise to follow this in due course with the formal three months' notice.

[1] Property in this context means 'legal ownership'.

[2] Churchwardens thus retain their powers of making 'presentments', and their duties in respect of answering the questions contained in the visitation articles and of attending visitations for the purpose of being admitted to office.

[3] 'Church trustees' originated from section 9 of the Compulsory Church Rates Abolition Act 1868, which gave power to appoint a body of trustees in any parish for the purpose of accepting, by bequest or otherwise, and of holding, any contributions which might be given to them for ecclesiastical purposes in the parish. Their powers included the investment of funds in their hands, accumulation of the income, and (subject to any conditions attached by the donors) power to pay over such funds to the churchwardens for expenditure on the ecclesiastical purposes of the parish.

The result of this present provision is that all the powers and functions of church trustees have passed to the parochial church council, and the church trustees and the power to appoint them have been swept away. Presumably, in the light of the fact that all the functions of the churchwardens in relation to the financial affairs of the Church have, under section 4(1)(ii)(a) *ante*, been transferred to the parochial church council, the council should itself apply any funds required for the ecclesiastical purposes of the parish, instead of paying them over to the churchwardens as section 9 of the Act of 1868 originally required.

or personal[1] relating to any powers duties or liabilities transferred to the council from the vestry churchwardens or church trustees as the case may be shall subject to the provisions of this Measure and so far as circumstances admit be construed as if any reference therein to the vestry or the churchwardens or church trustees referred to the council to which such powers duties or liabilities have been transferred and the said enactments shall be construed with such modifications as may be necessary for carrying this Measure into effect.

(3) Where any property is applicable to purposes connected with any such powers duties or liabilities as aforesaid, any deed or instrument which could be or could have been made or executed in relation to such property by a vestry, or by churchwardens or church trustees, may be made or executed by the council of the parish concerned.

(4) This Measure shall not affect any enactment in any private or local Act of Parliament under the authority of which church rates[2] may be made or levied in lieu of or in consideration of the extinguishment or of the appropriation to any other purpose of any tithes customary payments or other property or charge upon property which tithes payments property or charge previously to the passing of such Act had been appropriated by law to ecclesiastical purposes or in consideration of the abolition of tithes in any place or upon any contract made or for good

[1] An Act affecting the whole or a considerable part of the realm is said to be a general Act, because it is of general application. A local Act is one which applies to a particular locality, and a personal (sometimes called 'private') Act is one which affects only a particular person or class of persons.

[2] The reference here is to those church rates, imposed by private or local Acts, which were excepted from abolition by the Compulsory Church Rates Abolition Act 1868; see section 4(1)(i) *ante* and the notes thereto. Since the Measure does not affect the enactments imposing such rates, they are still to be levied by the authority originally empowered to do so, and not by the parochial church council.

or valuable consideration given and every such enactment shall continue in force in the same manner as if this Measure had not been passed.

For the purposes of this subsection 'ecclesiastical purposes' shall mean the building rebuilding enlargement and repair of any church or chapel and any purpose to which by common[1] or ecclesiastical law a church rate is applicable or any of such purposes.

Holding of property for ecclesiastical purposes: educational schemes.

5. (1) Subject to the provisions of this Measure, the council of every parish shall have power to acquire (whether by way of gift or otherwise) any property real or personal[2]—

(*a*) For any ecclesiastical purpose affecting the parish or any part thereof;

(*b*) For any purpose in connection with schemes (hereinafter called 'educational schemes') for providing facilities for the spiritual moral and physical training of persons residing in or near the parish.

(2) Subject to the provisions of this Measure and of the general law and to the provisions of any trusts affecting any such property, the council shall have power to manage, administer and dispose of any property acquired under this section.

(3) A council shall have power, in connection with any educational scheme, to constitute or participate in the constitution of a body of managers or trustees or a managing

[1] The common law is that part of the law of England, other than statute, which has existed continually since before legal memory. 'Ecclesiastical law' is a vague phrase, but it would certainly include the canon law which, so far as it binds the laity, has long ago become incorporated in the common law or in Acts of Parliament.

[2] All property is in law divided into real and personal property. The distinction is technical, but it may be taken that the two classes together embrace every kind of property.

committee consisting either wholly or partly of persons appointed by the council, and may confer on any such body or committee such functions in regard to the implementation of the scheme, and such functions relating to property held for the purposes of the scheme, as the council thinks expedient.

(4) The powers of a council with respect to educational schemes shall be exercised subject to and in accordance with the terms of any undertaking which may have been given by the council to the Secretary of State for Education and Science, Secretary of State for Wales or to any local authority in connection with any financial or other assistance given by the Secretary of State or the authority in relation to the scheme.

(5) A council shall not exercise any of its powers in relation to educational schemes without the consent of the diocesan education committee of the diocese, and any such consent may be given upon such terms and conditions as the committee considers appropriate in all the circumstances of the case.

In this subsection the expression 'diocesan education committee' includes any body of persons whether incorporated or not for the time being having the functions of such a committee by virtue of the Diocesan Education Committees Measure, 1955, and any orders made thereunder.

Supplementary provisions relating to certain property.

6. (1) After the commencement of this Measure,[1] a council shall not acquire any interest in land (other than a short lease as hereinafter defined) or in any personal property to be held on permanent trusts, without the consent of the diocesan authority.[2]

(2) Where, at or after the commencement of this

[1] i.e. the 2nd January 1957: see section 10(2) *post*.
[2] See section 1, p. 139 *ante*.

Measure, a council holds or acquires an interest in land (other than a short lease as hereinafter defined) or any interest in personal property to be held on permanent trusts, such interest shall be vested in the diocesan authority subject to all trusts, debts and liabilities affecting the same, and all persons concerned shall make or concur in making such transfers (if any) as are requisite for giving effect to the provisions of this subsection.

(3) Where any property is vested in the diocesan authority pursuant to subsection (2) of this section, the council shall not sell, lease, let, exchange, charge or take any legal proceedings with respect to the property without the consent of the authority; but save as aforesaid, nothing in this section shall affect the powers of the council in relation to the management, administration or disposition of any such property.

(4) Where any property is vested in the diocesan authority pursuant to subsection (2) of this section, the council shall keep the authority indemnified in respect of:

(*a*) all liabilities subject to which the property is vested in the authority or which may thereafter be incident to the property;
(*b*) all rates, taxes, insurance premiums and other outgoings of whatever nature which may from time to time be payable in respect of the property;
(*c*) all costs, charges and expenses incurred by the authority in relation to the acquisition or insurance of the property or as trustee thereof;
(*d*) all costs, proceedings, claims and demands in respect of any of the matters hereinbefore mentioned.

(5) The consents required by subsection (3) of this section are additional to any other consents required by law, either from the Charity Commissioners or the Secretary of State for Education and Science, Secretary of State for Wales or otherwise.

(6) In this section the expression 'short lease' means a

lease for a term not exceeding one year, and includes any tenancy from week to week, from month to month, from quarter to quarter, or from year to year.

(7) Any question as to whether personal property is to be held on permanent trusts shall be determined for the purposes of this section by a person appointed by the bishop.

Miscellaneous powers of Council.

7. The council of every parish shall have the following powers in addition to any powers conferred by the Constitution or otherwise by this Measure:—

(i) Power to frame an annual budget of moneys required for the maintenance of the work of the Church in the parish and otherwise and to take such steps as they think necessary for the raising collecting and allocating of such moneys;

(ii) Power to make levy and collect a voluntary church rate for any purpose connected with the affairs of the church including the administrative expenses of the council and the costs of any legal proceedings;[1]

(iii) Power jointly with the minister to appoint and dismiss the parish clerk and sexton or any persons performing or assisting to perform the duties of parish clerk or sexton and to determine their salaries and the conditions of the tenure of their offices or of their employment but subject to the rights of any persons holding the said offices at the appointed day;[2]

[1] This is a new power to levy a voluntary church rate, additional to the power to levy such a rate which has been transferred from the vestry to the council; see section 4(1)(i) *ante*, and the notes thereto. The purposes for which a rate may be levied under the new power would appear to be somewhat wider than those for which a rate may be levied under the transferred power.

[2] See Chapter 9 *ante*. The expression 'appointed day' presumably means the 1st July 1921, which is the 'relevant date' as defined by section 1 of the Measure.

(iv) Power jointly with the minister to determine the objects to which all moneys to be given or collected in church shall be allocated subject to the directions contained in the Book of Common Prayer as to the disposal of money given at the offertory;[1]

(v) Power to make representations to the bishop with regard to any matter affecting the welfare of the church in the parish.[2]

Accounts of the Council.

8. (1) Every council shall furnish to the annual church meeting the audited accounts of the council for the year ending on the 31st December immediately preceding the meeting and an audited statement of the funds and property, if any, remaining in the hands of the council at that date.

(2) At least seven days before the annual parochial church meeting, the council shall cause a copy of the said audited accounts and a copy of the said statement to be affixed at or near the principal door of the parish church as required by paragraph (2) of Rule 8 of the Church Representation Rules.[3]

(3) The accounts and statement shall be submitted to the meeting for approval, and, if approved, they shall be signed by the chairman of the meeting who shall then deliver them

[1] The directions appearing in the Book of Common Prayer which relate to the disposal of money have, by Canon B17A, ceased to have effect. The position now is that the council, jointly with the incumbent, is responsible for the money collected at all services.

[2] This places the council in the same position as an individual parishioner who *may* make such representations. In certain circumstances (see p. 74 *ante*) the churchwardens are under a duty to do so.

[3] See p. 100 *ante*.

to the council for publication, and the council shall forthwith cause them to be published in the manner provided by the Church Representation Rules.[1]

(4) The accounts of all trusts administered by the council shall be laid before the Diocesan Authority[2] annually.

Powers of bishop.

9. (1) The bishop may subject to the provisions of this Measure and the Constitution[3] make rules for carrying this Measure into effect within the diocese.

(2) If any act required by this Measure to be done by any person is not done within such time as the bishop may consider reasonable it may be done by or under the authority of the bishop.

(3) In the event of a council and a minister being unable to agree as to any matter in which their agreement or joint action is required under the provisions of this Measure, such matter shall be dealt with or determined in such manner as the bishop may direct.

(4) During a vacancy in a diocesan see the powers conferred upon the bishop by this section may be exercised by the guardian of the spiritualities.[4]

Short title, commencement, extent and repeals.

10. (1) This Measure may be cited as the Parochial Church Councils (Powers) Measure 1956.

(2) This Measure shall come into operation on the second day of January 1957.

[1] Now Rule 8(3) of the Church Representation Rules; see p. 101 *ante*.

[2] See section 1, p. 139 *ante*.

[3] The 'Constitution' means the Constitution of the Church Assembly (now the General Synod) appended to the Church of England Assembly (Powers) Act 1919.

[4] See pp. 1, 2 *ante*.

(3) This Measure shall extend to the whole of the Provinces of Canterbury and York except the Channel Islands and the Isle of Man:

Provided that, if an Act of Tynwald so provides, this Measure shall extend to the Isle of Man subject to such modifications, if any, as may be specified in such Act of Tynwald.

(4) The Parochial Church Councils (Powers) Measure, 1921, and the Parochial Church Councils (Powers) (Amendment) Measure, 1949, are hereby repealed.

(4) PROVISIONS OF PASTORAL MEASURE 1983 AS TO CHURCH MEETINGS AND COUNCILS IN CERTAIN CASES[1]

SCHEDULE 3

4.—(1) Where a pastoral scheme establishes a team ministry, the scheme, or the bishop's licence of any vicar in the team ministry, may assign to any such vicar the duties or a share in the duties of the chairmanship of the annual parochial church meeting and the parochial church council of the parish or any of the parishes in the area of the benefice for which the team ministry is established, and other duties of the minister of the parish under the Church Representation Rules,[2] or a share in such other duties, and the said Rules shall have effect accordingly:

Provided that, if the said duties of chairmanship are to be shared, the arrangements shall be such that the chairman on any occasion is determined in advance so that, in his

[1] The provisions in question are those contained in Schedule 3, paragraph 4 (relating to team and group ministries), paragraph 12 (relating to new parishes), and paragraph 13 (relating to united benefices and benefices held in plurality). The text of all three paragraphs is here set out.

[2] See the parts of the Church Representation Rules set out at p. 87 *et seq., ante.*

absence, the vice-chairman[1] of the parochial church council shall take the chair in accordance with the said Rules.

(2) Where a pastoral scheme establishes a team ministry for the area of a benefice which comprises a parish in which there are two or more churches or places of worship, the scheme may make provision, or authorise the bishop by instrument under his hand with the concurrence of the rector to make provision,—

(*a*) for ensuring due representation of the congregation of each such church or place of worship on the parochial church council of the parish,
(*b*) for the election of a district church council for any district in the parish in which such church or place of worship is situated and for the constitution, chairmanship and procedure of that council,
(*c*) for the functions of the parochial church council of the parish which must or may be delegated to the district church council,
(*d*) for the election or choice of deputy churchwardens for such church or place of worship and for the functions of churchwardens of the parish which must or may be delegated to the deputy churchwardens,

being provisions to the same effect as those which may be made by a scheme under the Church Representation Rules in the like case.

In this sub-paragraph 'place of worship' means a building or part of a building licensed for public worship according to the rites and ceremonies of the Church of England.

(3) Where a pastoral scheme establishes a team ministry for the area of a benefice which comprises more than one parish, the scheme may make provision, or authorise the

[1] The vice-chairman is always a layman: Church Representation Rules, Appendix II, paragraph 1(b) (p. 113 *ante*).

bishop by instrument under his hand with the concurrence of the rector to make provision,—

(*a*) for the establishment of a team council,
(*b*) for the chairmanship, meetings and procedure of the team council, and
(*c*) for the functions of the parochial church council of each parish in the area which must or may be delegated to the team council,

being provisions to the same effect as those which may be made by a scheme under the Church Representation Rules in the like case.

(4) Where a pastoral scheme establishes a group ministry, the scheme may make provision, or authorise the bishop by instrument under his hand with the concurrence of all the members of the group to make provision,

(*a*) for the establishment of a group council,
(*b*) for the chairmanship, meetings and procedure of the group council, and
(*c*) for the functions of the parochial church council of each parish in the area for which the group ministry is established which must or may be delegated to the group council,

being provisions to the same effect as those which may be made by a scheme under the Church Representation Rules in the like case.

(5) Any provisions which are included in a pastoral scheme or the bishop's instrument by virtue of sub-paragraph (2), (3) or (4) shall cease to have effect[1] at the expiration of such period as may be specified in the scheme or instrument, as the case may be, being a period which

[1] When the provisions mentioned in sub-paragraph 5 cease to have effect, the normal procedure would be to replace them with a scheme made under rules 16, 17A, or 17B of the Church Representation Rules; see p. 110 *et seq.*, *ante*.

does not exceed five years from the date of the establishment of the team ministry or group ministry to which the pastoral scheme or instrument relates, and that period may not be extended or renewed by a subsequent scheme or instrument of the bishop.

(6) Any provisions which were included in a pastoral scheme or bishop's instrument by virtue of sub-paragraph (2) or (4), as originally enacted,[1] shall cease to have effect at the expiration of whichever of the following periods last expires, that is to say, the period of five years beginning with the date of the establishment of the team ministry or group ministry to which the scheme or instrument relates and the period of three years beginning with the date on which this Measure comes into operation.

12.—(1) A pastoral scheme which creates a new parish may make provision, or authorise the bishop by instrument under his hand to make provision, for ensuring that the congregation of every church or place of worship in the new parish will have its own elected representatives of the laity on the parochial church council of that parish.

(2) Any provision included in a pastoral scheme or the bishop's instrument by virtue of sub-paragraph (1) shall cease to have effect at the expiration of such period as may be specified in the scheme or instrument, as the case may be, being a period which does not exceed five years beginning with the date on which the new parish comes into being, and that period may not be extended or renewed by a subsequent pastoral scheme or instrument of the bishop.[2]

(3) Any such provision shall have effect notwithstanding anything in the Church Representation Rules.

[1] i.e. as Schedule 3, paragraph 3, sub-paragraphs (2) and (4) of the Pastoral Measure 1968.

[2] Once the period of up to five years has expired, the position is governed by the Church Representation Rules, p. 87 *et seq., ante*.

(4) Without prejudice to any general rule of law relating to parochial church councils, the powers, duties and liabilities set out in section 4(1)(ii) of the Parochial Church Councils (Powers) Measure 1956[1] shall continue to apply to any church which was formerly a parish church and becomes a chapel of ease as the result of a pastoral scheme or order, and to the churchyard of any such church, except so far as the scheme or order otherwise provides.

13.—(1) Where a pastoral scheme provides for two or more parishes to be comprised in the area of a single benefice or a pastoral scheme or order provides for two or more benefices to be held in plurality, the scheme or order may make provision, or authorise the bishop by instrument under his hand with the concurrence of the incumbent of the benefice or benefices to make provision,—

(*a*) for establishing a joint parochial church council for all or some of the parishes of the benefice or benefices;
(*b*) for the chairmanship, meetings and procedure of that council; and
(*c*) for the functions of the parochial church council of any such parish which must or may be delegated to the joint parochial church council,

being provisions to the same effect as those which may be made by a scheme under Church Representation Rules in the like case.

(2) Subject to sub-paragraph (4), any provisions which are included in a pastoral scheme or order or the bishop's instrument by virtue of sub-paragraph (1) shall cease to have effect[2] at the expiration of such period as may be specified in the scheme, order or instrument, being a

[1] See p. 142 *ante*.
[2] When the provisions mentioned in sub-paragraph 2 cease to have effect, the normal procedure would be to replace them with a scheme made under rule 17 of the Church Representation Rules; see p. 113 *ante*.

period which does not exceed five years from the date on which the scheme or order, as the case may be, came into operation, and that period may not be extended or renewed by a subsequent pastoral scheme, pastoral order or instrument of the bishop.

(3) Subject to sub-paragraph (4), any provisions which were included in a pastoral scheme or order by virtue of this paragraph as originally enacted,[1] shall cease to have effect at whichever of the following periods last expires, that is to say, the period of five years beginning with the date of the establishment of the joint parochial church council to which the scheme or order relates and the period of three years beginning with the date on which this Measure comes into operation.

(4) Where the provisions of a pastoral scheme or order for the holding of benefices in plurality are terminated under section 18(2), any provision of a pastoral scheme or order or the bishop's instrument establishing a joint parochial church council for all or some of the parishes of those benefices and the other provisions thereof affecting that council shall cease to have effect on the date on which the first mentioned provisions cease to have effect.

[1] i.e. Schedule 3, paragraph 13 of the Pastoral Measure 1968.

11

Conduct of Meetings

The preceding chapters of this book have been designed with a view to placing the rights and duties of the laity in the parishes in their proper and larger context of the Church of which they are members, and to affording guidance to them in the interpretation of their position, especially in the light of modern legislation.

In this concluding chapter some attempt is made to assist them in the normal conduct of their business, particularly in parochial church councils.

The chairman of the council is normally the incumbent of the parish, but in his absence or on his invitation his place is taken by a lay vice-chairman elected by the council. The incumbent is a member of all committees of the council, but not necessarily the chairman of a committee.

The incumbent is primarily responsible for convening parochial church meetings and the parochial church council. In particular, he is under a legal duty to convene the annual parochial church meeting not later than the 30th April in every year, and at least four meetings of the parochial church council during the year. The provisions of the Church Representation Rules as to the notices of meetings[1] which must be given should be strictly observed; otherwise

[1] See pp. 98, 135 *ante*.

there is a risk of the proceedings at meetings being invalidated. The incumbent should instruct the secretary as to the form of agenda which is to be sent to the members.

Before the meeting of a parochial church council, the chairman should already have perused the draft minutes of the last meeting, the reading of which should be the first item of the agenda after prayers have been said. They should be compiled by the secretary from notes taken at the time, and should, before the meeting, have been submitted to the incumbent for his comments. In their final draft form they should be written in the minute book. It is important to remember that the minutes are intended to be a record of business transacted. It is unnecessary and sometimes inconvenient to give a detailed account of a discussion. The minutes should state, for example, that Mr. A. proposed, and Mr. B. seconded, a resolution (which should be set out in full). If an amendment is proposed and seconded, it should be similarly recorded. The minutes may state the name of any person who spoke in a debate, but this is not necessary. But it should be recorded, e.g., that a resolution or an amendment was carried (or defeated) and the number of votes given on either side in a division should always be stated. It is expressly provided by the rules that if one-fifth of the members of a parochial church council present and voting on a resolution so require, the minutes should record the names of those voting for and against the resolution; also that any member is entitled to require the manner in which his vote was cast to be recorded.[1]

The names of those present at a meeting should always be recorded.

When the minutes have been read, the chairman should ask if they are a correct record. This is not an invitation to discuss the merits of what is recorded but merely to obtain agreement that the record is correct. If exception is taken as

[1] See p. 137 *ante*.

to the accuracy of the record, that question may be debated and the council may vote either to accept the record or to amend it.

The chairman should then ask the council for authority to sign the minutes as read, or as amended, and when he has done so, they become the authentic account of the transactions recorded therein, and are receivable in evidence in any court of justice, if produced to that court by the chairman or secretary.

At this stage it is customary to deal with any business arising out of the minutes, other than business which forms a separate item on the agenda. After this has been disposed of, any correspondence received by the secretary (including apologies for non-attendance) should be read and the instructions of the council taken thereon.

Then the other items on the agenda are taken, one by one, and the decision of the council upon each of them arrived at. Voting is by a show of hands, and a resolution is decided by a simple majority of those present and voting, the chairman having a second or casting vote.

It is customary to include at the end of an agenda paper an item called 'Other Business', It is within the competence of the council to deal with a matter not specifically mentioned on the agenda paper but the Rules require that three-quarters of the members present at the meeting must consent; and even if such consent is forthcoming, the chairman might reasonably, when the matter is important, rule that it is to be adjourned to a future meeting.

It is open to any member, at any stage in the proceedings, to raise a point of order. In doing so he must confine his remarks to the point of order; he should not be allowed to discuss the merits of the matter under debate. Thus it is in order to submit to the chairman that the matter is not one which it is within the competence of the meeting to discuss, but it is not in order to raise *in this way* the question of the expediency of such a discussion.

The decision whether the question is or is not a point of

order rests with the chairman and he must decide it. When he has given his decision it must be accepted by the meeting.

Any member may address the council, but unless he is given leave he should not normally speak more than once in relation to the particular matter under discussion. But he should always be allowed to make an explanation or correction of what he has previously said, should he feel that this is desirable in the light of what is said by a member speaking subsequently to him. The chairman may not properly refuse to hear a member, but he has the right to decide on the order in which members may speak, and he may in a proper case stop any member who in his opinion is speaking irrelevantly to the matter under discussion.

If a point of order is raised, the chairman must first make up his mind that it really is a point of order. If he considers that it is, he must decide the point of order at once, i.e. before the general discussion is resumed.

Index